IN THE VALLEY OF SHADO

First published in Great Britain
by The Diamond Press
5, Berners Mansions
34-6 Berners St
London W1

Typeset by Grassroots Typeset
364A Regents Park Rd, N3
Printed & bound by Whitstable Litho, Kent

IN THE VALLEY OF SHADOW
(a ciné-poem-cum-fantasy)

DIVINATIONS

books four & five

JAY RAMSAY

THE DIAMOND PRESS
LONDON

Printed on 100% recycled
Five Seasons book paper

CONTENTS

IN THE VALLEY OF SHADOW
(a ciné-poem-cum-fantasy)

DIVINATIONS (book 5)

prelude

elemental

IN THE TEMPLE OF SUN

in the year of light

The unknown in the future in the shadow of a thundercloud.

I am drawn, dragged towards it: as ever.

I must see the lightening.

Hail falling in extraordinary large frozen pellets. The daffodil heads bob, struck. The grass spreads, pocked with instant snow. Spring is in confusion. And this fear, come out of nowhere, making me listen. Waking me, wide awake. My voice speeds up as I move to turn round and speak. It tastes like sleep on my tongue. We can only dream when we speak.

The hail falls into my outstretched palms. I am a child trying to hold water in my hands, watching it trickle away through my clenched fingers. The thunder cannons, rolling like a huge metal ball. A streak of forked light flashes down, parting the air...and the thought, thought by the time it has already gone invisible...lit up, for a second and then vanishing, in this image you are standing in

Me also: me nothing: me speak in my only freedom - sound.

Like drowning. In air. Everything I have seen crowds my mind's screen. Tangled brilliant colours shifting and changing, as the light does, faster even...images and places and faces swirling, torn shreds of silk, never adequately expressed, never wholly: so you are drawn on, teased, tested, tempted. Every possibility of sensitivity becomes you. There is no escape. You feel yourself enough without being able to end, cut, curtail yourself.

How can you end all this feeling? the dark cloud is vast; but there is light in front outside the window, slowly brightening. There is no barrier between me and it. And no way I can hide from it. I am alive and I am open, I am bathed and broken; my bones blanch in this hunched over sitting shape

To be a ray of sunlight. To be light

Shining on my face and closed eyes as its rhythm moves through me, seen through, in pools of pure reflection my voice enters. The sound of the sea fills me, and my brain is a lighthouse turning among fringes of wings and piercing gulls' cries

And it is ready for us and our traces. To flood in deep and wide leaving a stretch of unmarked sunlit sand. That is renewed, again, perpetually. In each of us. And as it ends, I am left gazing into this one long moment as the liquid fire of eye-mirroring earth comes together in the only thing that I can possess.

My death.

10

IN THE VALLEY OF SHADOW

(a ciné-poem-cum-fantasy)

for the Shadow Master

'Build then the ship of death, for you must take
the longest journey, to oblivion.

And die the death, the long and painful death
that lies between the old self and the new'

- D.H. Lawrence

'Most of our contemporaries never get out of the tunnel'

- Arthur Koestler

'This is the place, this is it, now or never - again.
Like the man said, some Viking in a tight saga,
One's back is bare without a brother, brother,
So keep me covered, I'm going in alone'

- Libby Houston

'Suddenly, I was in a very dark, very deep valley. It was as though there
was a pathway, almost a road, through the valley, and I was going down
the path...Later, after I was well, the thought came to me, 'Well, now
I know what the Bible means by 'the valley of the shadow of death',
because I've been there'

- quoted in Dr Raymond Moody's *Life After Life*

(*and so...*

```
                    ┌─────────────────┐
                    │                 │
                    │                 │
                    │      intro      │
                    │                 │
                    │                 │
                    └─────────────────┘
```

Begin.Begun.Begin.Begun.Begin.Begun.How may times? did the pitch
black dark door slam back in your face? consider. Abandon All Hope
Ye Who Enter Here (Into The City Of Dreadful Night). Listen - I'll tell
you. There is no way in because you are already here...

a. Black screen. Silence. Very slowly in the blackness, tiny points of light
    begin to emerge. They brighten as stars. They fade, one by one, to
    the sound of dripping water

b. Music: sombre, rhythmic, building from a bass riff. Aerial shot of
    London. Lit buildings, streets, and the traffic moving over one of the
    bridges across the dark river

c. Cut to descending spiral escalator staircase. A blind man, clutching
    at the rail, moves down, step by step, holding his white stick out in
    front of him with his free hand

c. contd...cut to platform. Steel rails leading into the tunnel. Sound of
    an approaching train. Music still. The train arrives, its twin lights loom-
    ing out of the blackness, blurring as it brakes and stops. The doors
    thump open.

c. contd...close shot of head and shoulders of an anonymous figure fac-
    ing the doors, about to board. Closens to the back of his head and
    the black hat he is wearing. Closens until the blackness blurs, and...

YOU'RE IN

falling, the spiral
beckoning, its deep whirlpool
turning ahead of you

with a a graceful bow, the diver's body plunges into the water clean into the eye of an enormous pupil

with a clumsy scuffle, the blind man's foot catches on the last of the stairs as he falls forwards, his stick rattling ahead of him

with a brown DHSS envelope poised on his knee, the poet (who is no one) begins to scribble a sequence of hasty and almost illegible notes

as the train pulls away with a dull heave

sunk, to a whisper
the head bent forward
the whole body as if
twice as heavy

falling

turned on feeling
like death in the throat
sucked into an empty space
where there are no words

falling)

'un dèreglement de tous ses sens'

(to reach the core, a glimmering black jewelled underground palace in
 which The Shadow lives

basement of the house
river of Lethe
& of Styx

his vision closed, he began to descend
into the pit of humanity

and oh the sadness
welling up from its depths like stale air

Do people really live down here? slumped on the benches, hidden in the niches, locked behind the passage doors the passengers never enter

as the train pauses beside an opening into the caked dusty wall where a ghostly pair of hands and a mouth are raised open

pressing his dissolving face against the smudged glass

Necropolis

huge head behind shades filling the whole space, with trains pouring in and out through its eyes

its body sunk in history, and each of us a cell in its -
cold brain dark heart and pitch black submerged genitalia

and the first circle of hell
is the dead mind:

Victorian

'Implacable November weather. As much mud in the streets, as if the waters had but newly retired from the face of the earth, and it would not be wonderful to meet a Megolosaurus, forty feet long or so, waddling like an elephantine lizard up Holborn Hill...
Fog everywhere...'

(...in a back street. The sound of horses' hooves on cobblestones. The carriage rattles by, briefly obscuring the shadow of a figure who is waiting under the dim glow of one of the street lamps. He is dressed as a gentleman, in top hat and cloak. He carries a black cane.

His face stays still in shadow. A woman comes forward into the dim circular glow. She is poorly dressed, with a shawl wrapped round her shoulders. Her damp red hair hangs down. Her eyes meet his, briefly. He walks a step forward, facing her, and then kisses her, abruptly, on the mouth. She takes his arm as they turn, and indicates a small lit window up the street in the direction she has just come from

these streets this city of memory
laden in the autumn air
leaf fall against the sun
a hundred years later
in the cemetery

Victorian, wandering
mute and nostalgic
'Come into the garden, Maud
 For the black bat, Night, has flown,
 Come into the garden, Maud,
 I am here at the gate alone'

her ghost hovering
her ghost quickening
come into the cemetery, my love
and we will make love among the stones

melancholic necrophiliac in necropolitan amour, buries his poems in a fit of despair in her grave

Echo, wasting away
till nothing is left but her voice
her bones changed into rocks

sitting on a tombstone, her legs curled under her, leaning to one side, gazing ahead: her headless hair superimposed onto a nearby bush

the twitter of birds
as the sunlight fades

her colour photo propped on the desk: framed in shadow with the window behind her, her hair loose, brown eyes, booted ankle crossed over her knee

his hand reaching up her skirt

touches the entrance

enters the water
the smell of it still
on his fingers

staring down into his lap as the train moves

sucks on the joint he has rolled out of lotus leaves

'till with the refluent dance she reappears'

...into the tunnel gathering speed
flash darkness as the carriage sways
and the lights teeter

his pen jogs
(his penis jissoms)

'So I returned. Our destiny is fell;
 For in this Limbo we must ever dwell,
 Shut out alike from Heaven and Earth and Hell'

LEICESTER SQUARE

eyes getting used to the dark...hearing voices

winding slowly
on the circling edge
with miles and miles of tunnel
left to the centre

this dark vein artery we white corpuscles queue along in
blood-flow and sweat-flow and shit-flow

the mind's flow melting
to its seven-eighths submerged

 - you name it if you can, I can't - it slips in my fingers like black soap

falling

its sings in my throat like a black bird
O darkling thrush on the eve of this century
the self unseeing and the woman calling

in the thick of the blind mind - that's it!

in this Victorian house of pain we live in

- the first of the inhabitants sits next door like Des Esseintes, reading De Sade. His lean sensitive sharp-featured face tips back another swig of Coke. His hand rustles in the crisp packet beside him. He is dressed in a pair of fake leopard skin trousers and a worn silk shirt. Around him, the room is a clutter of magazines and comics. The walls are bare. A single naked bulb hangs from the ceiling. A steel string guitar lies face down on the unmade bed. The television in front of him is propped on a chair. He is watching a video of himself moving around a beautifully furnished *fin de siècle* room)

'Hi. Had a good time?'
'Yeah. I went to see that woman up in Highgate'
'Oh, right'
'Have you got the sugar?'
'No, Fiona has'
'OK. See you'
'Ciao'

the blind man

BLINDNESS CAN ARRIVE GRADUALLY. YEAR BY YEAR, DAY BY DAY, THE VISION SLOWLY FADES...

I don't know. Everything's black, that's all. I am the witness. 'I wasn't ready for it. Nothing seemed real. At first, I could barely imagine the lawn and the trees. There were gaps everywhere. My brain reeled from the effort of filling them. Everything was strange. I felt the grass, but it wasn't the same grass as I had seen. Everything was abstract, too. It felt as if my personality had gone...

(casting a white fly blindly
 into this pool of darkness beneath me

reading and writing were what went first. My central vision. The lines began to amalgamate in front of my eyes. I began seeing people obliquely and spasmodically, like patches in the midst of a blacked out tissue. I became increasingly aware of my solitude. Everyone was on the other side of the partition'

...and seeing nothing
I am all ear
I am touch

I am listening
through all of this
my voice whispers
its deep black seam

threading along the passageways
burrowing under the mountain
in the tread of my dissolving steps

towards his reflection
the point where all
our lines meet

where we meet as we are
in the dark

I hear a room full of people humming in the darkness

I, Tiresias
I am the heart's eye
I am a slow worm singing in the fire
(the soft one, the slow step, the soul thread)

blind eye

blind side
blind track
blind ditch
blind stitch
blind alley
blind drunk
blind man's buff

blind man's holiday
(before the candles are lit)
blind coal/anthracite
(burning without flame)
blind worm, slow worm
(with a very small eye)

window blinds
(black out at wartime)

mmmmmmmmmmmmmmmmm

the sound rising
the brief calm deepening
pausing on the edge
of this descending circle)

There are days here so dark, you cannot tell where the sky ends and the
sea begins

I was on night patrol. The explosion almost made me jump out of my
body. The next thing I knew, I was on a stretcher on the way to Tangiers

(Aesop p.187 - the blind man's touch

A dog outside barking like a saw at its own echo

when the dead come out
at the end of summer,
bones in a desert
bodies in a park

aubade

But what I wanted to tell you was: the blind black lady that always walks

along the street wearing a black fur and carrying a black handbag, you
know? Well I saw her twice today. This morning, going into Andy's like
she usually does for her tea; and then this afternoon, I just happened
to glance out of the window (I think it must have been just after you
went to the laundrette) and I saw her walking along, effortlessly, smiling,
carrying a baby

thin green
thread of hope
glimpsing the end
the seed that will hold
the tree that will become of it

At Binsey Church (near where they cut the poplars down), the inscription
tells the story of Alfgur's suit to Frideswide, who rejects him. Alfgur
continues his lustings until he is struck blind by a flash of lightning.
Frideswide prays to St. Mark Of Antioch, who appears to her in a vision
and instructs her to strike the ground with her staff. On doing so, water
gushed out of the soil, bathing Alfgur's eyes and restoring his sight. And
so, clearly seeing the folly of his ways, he returned to Oxford a happier
and a wiser man

silent among the graves
and then stooping by the well
asking only for the truth

the way water
is constantly seeking a lower level

I am the watcher
I journey inside him
I am the old man he dreamt of on the summer road

groping down the stairs in the darkness for a piss
(echoes of Robert Fripp behind the door's lit frame)

the blind look of seeing oneself looking

'In numerous cultures blindness is a supreme infirmity and abdication
  from life - in Greek mythology the poet and the seer are blind so that
  they may, by the antennae of speech, see further'

blind lips
blind hands

a blind date
with fate

his white stick tapping the way
his bowed head the story of our days

'In the Valley Of The Blind the behaviour of the sighted man was strange,
 so he was to be blinded, and he fled to the hills'

A UNIQUE EXPERIENCE FOR THE BLIND at South Kensington Natural
History Museum. The exhibition is specially designed for the blind and
the partially sighted. (The image we have used to advertize this event
depicts a blind girl standing by a stuffed lion, her hand resting on the
edge of the lion's open mouth

and afterwards,
is it imagineable?

as I speak all of what I have into this dictaphone)

'If cured of blindness, the subject finds it difficult to recognize patterns
 and faces, and orient in space'

(will I live to see
 those thousand birds
 wheeling over the Sahara?

straining from his pent up box of flesh towards a white light he would
bathe and swim and surface and stand and dance in)

'as a deeper blindness closed in on him'

```
 ┌─────────────────────┐
 │                     │
 │        war          │
 │                     │
 └─────────────────────┘
```

'And Germany's place in the new European balance of power created
 by her victory in 1870 was also determined by -

War!
that's what we need to wake up the nation
War!
come on, boys, lets have no more *philandering about*. Your country is
at war! wake up, wake up, get those feet moving, one two, one two,
forward, march!

Private Jenkins, this isn't a time for *dreaming*. Private Jenkins, why do
your boots not shine like black suns? Private Jenkins, why do you
inwardly retch at the thought of trapping a fellow human being like a
helpless bird in your gunsights?

oh oh oh what a lovely...
thundering of doomed hooves
as into the Valley Of Death
rode the six hundred

oh oh oh what a lovely
piece of violent shit is Man
what darkness drives him
to this insanity

what deep blood lust
shuddering through him
staring out from his eyes?
Private Jenkins!

You're in the army now
- what invisible hand
tweaking eyes and mouth and

wire-strung shoulders?

what machine, forcing itself
up through his anus
like a clambering tank?
oh oh oh

I remember. There was some heavy artillery to start with to 'soften things
up'. Essentially, it was Hay's New Army against the Kaiser's New Army.
When the massacre began, a feeling of enormous despair took hold of
me. I saw the overwhelming pointlessness of it all. I saw men falling
in hundreds, collapsing like wheat. Something strange was happening
to me. I couldn't hear anything, and everything I was seeing filled my
field of vision in silent slow motion

...close-up of man running. An animated sequence of stills. No sound.
Trenches behind him. Trenches in front of him. As he runs, the mud
splashing under his feet, he wrestles with the gun slung over his shoulder,
pushing it aside. Twenty yards to go. His arms begins to spread. A bright
light closens towards him. His arms spread, his muddy face and hair tip-
ped back...freeze

the crackling wireless-voice 'Good evening, this is the Home Service'
detailing Hitler's speech to Germany

come on boys
'Its a new sensation...'
'A marvellous creation...'
do the - goosestep, c'mon, yeah

Adolf, with toothbrush moustache and electric guitar with Eva on backing
vocals

Got mit uns, mein Feurher
what a stange parody
of this emblem
twisted into a swastika?

I'll tell you: this circle is populated by those who pledged themselves
to the autonomy of the human mind, disavowing any divine connection.
The result is inevitably a spiritual nightmare

Adolf sings hymn number 2001 ('Only A Sudden And Violent Solution
Is Possible')

probably best described as a kind of primal sexual urge seeking
sublimation through intercourse with destruction

ah yes, Herr Freud, very inter-esting

The photograph shows Hitler looking grimly triumphant, Mussolini and
Goering grinning, and Chamberlain and Daladier looking sheepish

I was giving a lecture at the time, and hearing the crunch of marching jack-
boots outside, I paused, and found myself saying very quietly and slowly

Doesn't our boy Patrick look like the kind of boy you'd be proud to have
for a son? Come on, boys, join the National Front

the Home Guard
poised with pitchforks and twelve-bores
watching the parachutist slowly descending
'Come for lunch, has he?'

the land map of Europe like a schizophrenic chessboard

Pawn to King 4: I demand my freedom (and the tower of the king begins
falling around him)

falling

asleep like Nostradamus
and dreams

300 deportees...Malthausen...Kara something-something mountains...
bored tunnel to give Panzers access to the Adriatic...flogged for any word
of sabotage...homosexual criminals, sadistic pleasure of guards...injection
of benzene into patient...watching the body burn...taking photos for his
wife

of a rage so great, it would envelop the earth if he uttered it
('the Nam films are nothing. Have you heard The Falklands Tapes?')
- bugger the Mary Rose, ay ay

imagine, a battlefield with a bloody *film crew* on it

documentary voices hammering in his ears

the brain bathed

in the blood of a fantasy
that is no fantasy at all

and dreams

of the exhibits in the Imperial War museum coming to Madame Tussaud-
like life

the brain bathed
with the madness
of a colossally broken sanity

'Don't cry for me, Eva Perona - fascist bitch!'
 (hisses the Argentinian in the Belsize Park *Pip*)

mmmm, delicious brain soup

and dreams

'On a moonlit night
 In a desert site
 I dreamt that war did cease,
 No fierce alarms
 Or clash of arms
 Disturb'd the wondrous peace'

on this violent and pathetic star

I was down at Land's End. The marines were landing. I stood watching
the battleships sailing out. Then I seemed to be somehow rising above
the ground, looking down, looking back on it all

as the wave fell
and became the Sergeant's
hand shaking me awake

Private Jenkins!
(Sergeant, this is tedious. Sergeant, this is unending)

round two! as they float out with their gloves raised

from Caesar to Churchill, it is all one war
(my love, my love will it ever end)

what earth
where we born for
to suffer like this?
what God
planned the script
for His Children to maim and mutilate and murder?

de profundis clamavi

This is out of my control

I wake to gunfire and the sound of a baby crying

It was hell. We were frozen, wading through rivers, tramping across the broken ground, with the desert wreckage behind us. Alamein, Fūka, and then the Mareth Line - we really thought the Germans had had it. Then we came to Monte Cassino

the battles engraved
name by name
on his kukri knife

Lt. Colonel, MC and bar, the pain of it haunting him forever
locked like his true voice deep inside him
'his calm bravery is something I can never forget'

There we were, dug in at the foot of it. The Germans were up in the old citadel, shelling us, hour after hour. Then it all went quiet. I thought they must have run out

the way his face
changed, his smile slowly vanished
he was only 19 and he looked ten years older

what dark voyeur
with his coin poised
peeps through the crack
with his hand down his trousers?

'The soldiers' cocks are a black burlesque
 They break my heart with what they say'

When I was a child

'When Tyson had left him there was silence; more complete silence than Peter had ever known. It seemed as though the eighteen feet of soil above his head was pressing down, pressing inwards. Then, in the silence he heard the faint hiss of air pushed by the man at the pump through its life-line of jam tins joined end to end. This metal pipe, coming along the upper tunnel, down the shaft and along the wall of the lower tunnel, was his connection with the outside world - that, and the rope which pulled the toboggan. He took the knife and began to hack away at the clay in front of him...'

I could hardly get the spade in the ground. In the end, I left him in a shallow grave covered over with stones. Less than a minute later, and it would have been me

'I don't want a holiday in the sun...
I want to see some his-tory'

It is something your generation finds difficult to understand

banned by the BBC
and now, twenty four years later
in a London library with the lights off
the makeshift screen and the hollow sound

this real unreal
dreaming wide awake

as they crouch in terror
under the shaking kitchen table
as the light bursts around them
and blazes white

It was a job I had to do as far as I was concerned. I could have been delivering a parcel

Hiroshima
Necropolis
Nagasaki
Necropolis

and the deathcloud
hanging over all of us
(a broken test tube
 a stained white laboratory coat)

and all from a walk one morning in the snow
the equation leaving them breathless with silence

as the drilling for a moment stops outside

and he falls on his back, the ringside around him
misting over his eyes as the count reaches ten

his blood beginning to still

and every poet on earth was silent

God save Ronald Reagan
Friggin' with his bomb
He weren't being wicked, God
'E knew right from wrong

sing it: Land of Dope and Gory

falling
        fading

the sleepers lined along the platform
huddled together and wrapped in blankets

the siren of death singing

wake up!

His hands and lips and frozen Russian face, his hair a fuzz of frost, his
deep-closed eyes and moustached mouth leaning forward weighed on
the back of his hand

shadowy figures
standing around him
silent in the whiteness

gazing at the page

fragments of Dresden
filling my mind
the burning city set
to the New World Symphony

History is an essay in pathology

Her father died in such a way her mother could not tell, and nor could
she imagine what kind of horror it was, and nor can we

Dachau
                    the slumped skinny skeletons
                                            and no birds sing

across the distance that seperates us from the heart of what we are

HAMMERSMITH

Story means to learn by studying. History means - to know

as the dot fades
into the centre of the TV set)

'shantih shantih shantih'

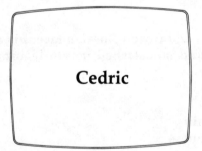

Cedric

(Good morning, machine. Bright morning, machine

This Is The Modern World

the madman

cum blindman
cum mask man rides into
chipper on his renovated
1938 bike, besuited
in tattered grey
paint-spattered overalls
the bike's thin rusted exhaust pipes
& huge mudguards

into the valley
downhill all the way

London swallowing him
in its sea of traffic
queuing past outside
the rush hour's myriad
alarm-clocked face
shrilling a million
working slaves into action

Wake up, Caliban, come on, get up and eat your Cornflakes
(*grunt*) 'Wha? time is't?'
'Time you were up, sir'
(*soft purring voice*)
'Ohjeesus'
(*scrambles out of bed, holding receiver*)
'Mr Caliban. This is is your employer speaking'
(*hard clipped tone*)

brushes the sleep
from his eyes
the morning light
falling across the carpet
the mess of books and papers
the still open copy of *Man As Machine*
face down on the eiderdown -
gropes for his glasses

and on the tube to work
staring rudely at a woman
glazed gazing company
of unisex exhaustion
hide behind a paper
flip open attaché case

skim from her returning eyes
his mannered face abruptly
preoccupied and thoughtful

Such a lovely girl, that answering machine...

Now: today's project is The Super Human Being

(*quick burst of futuristic music*)

I don't know why you think this is funny. I'm quite serious. We are going
to build an *indomitable creature*. Now. My name is Mr Skinner

you rat
with your steely eyes
staring out of a rat's skin

'The brain is a curious item which lives on a variety of intellectual picture
 food, and dies in complete darkness of itself'

whereas
this machine
is immortal!
(and strictly masculine)

Now: whereas this piece of childish science fiction (*indicating a dalek
behind him and the lectern, downstage left*) is merely a humorous travesty
of our actual potential - *as machines*, I mean - on my right, just coming
through the door now (*gestures, beckoning with his finger*) is something
I think you will find rather more recognizable and impressive

Good morning, Cedric. *Good morning, Mr Skinner*

Now: Cedric is here this morning with the special permission of the Inter-
national Federation Of Behavioural Brain Surgeons. Cedric nods, his smile
rippling in a row of flickering lights. Speaks: *it is a privelege, sir*. Now:
Cedric, as you can see, is built as a fully functioning adult. His pro-
gramme, installed in the latest microfiche, carries all twenty six volumes
of the Encyclopaedia Brittanica as well as the Complete Works of the
Elizabethan King of Soap Opera, William Shakespeare. Cedric responds
instantly: '*To be or not to be*'. Indeed, Cedric. Now: Cedric was con-
structed from a basic control head blueprint which I devised as a result
of my entensive study of rats, and I'd like to take the opportunity now
to thank all those poor dumb sub-animal creatures who kindly submitted

to my machinations in the name of science (*loud applause*). What these rats taught me was that if you put a human brain in a maze, at the centre of which is a concealed reward (a piece of arsenic-laced cheese, for example), the brain will register a little thrill of delight, or consciousness as we call it. Now: when Cedric was still at the four wheeled stage (*Cedric sighs and fidgets*), I programmed him to give a hoot when he reached the reward I gave him. Cedric? Cedric is rather shy, I'm afraid. Do you remember what it was, Cedric? *A pocket calculator, sir*. Very good, Cedric. Now: as Cedric will dimly recall in his infantile retrieval system, he began as a metal box with two sensors placed either side of it. Later, these became his eyes. From the word go (which we key in as 'enter', as some of you may know) me and my colleagues realized that it was a relatively short step (relatively speaking) from identifying the basic constituents of a human being, to translating those constituents into functioning parts that would finally be capable of self-directed movement. But first we needed to design a central processor which was able to store and reproduce all the necessary correlates of the nervous system as a series of simple synthetic actions. To start with, of course, all this had to operate on a purely mental or 'metal' level. In terms of consciousness, of course, the transfer was quite simple. The difficulty lay in translating the essentials from their behaviourial counterparts into precise mathematical language; and for this purpose we used Boolean Algebra as our base. Thus (*writes on his overhead projector*), for instance

$$\text{ABC: A (not A): A and B} \rightarrow \text{A} \cap \text{B/A} \cup \text{B}$$

the individual element (symbolized by Cedric) belonging to class A. Equally, what we designate as

$$\text{A} \cap \text{B}$$

represents class inclusion whereby the individual (A) is related to the sum of what he is programmed as (B). (*Cedric's eyes narrow attentively*). Now, we can represent this interaction through a Venn diagram in which both A and B intersect, at the point of their intersection which represents what is called the nil class, or zero in plain Esperanto. In other words, basing Cedric's consciousness on the human biodegradeable model, his centre is nil, or nothing. He is basically nothing. Cedric's existence as a being only comes into operation when we consider his interaction with B (the sum of his programmed parts, or his 'identity'). The rectangle, surrounding A and B on all four sides, symbolizes 'everything', or the world of stimuli and its subconscious levels we experience as varying degrees of neurofantastical response bubbles, or 'dreams' as they are commonly referred to. $\cap$ and U represent, respectively, the processes of conjunction and disjunction through which all mechanical phenomena relate, and in the brain through the feedback reflex we call information. Add to this the basic minimum of emotional requirements (the icing on the cake, so to speak), symbolized by, for instance

$$C = \text{choice}$$
$$NC = \text{no choice}$$

and you have what is essentially any human being in a cybernetic nutshell (*takes a deep satisfied breath*). Now: to bring Cedric up to scratch as a responsive entity, we were then confronted by the exciting prospect of hearing Cedric's first words! (*brief pause*). Having encoded his basic linguistic patterning in a devious mixture of Algol, Cobol and Fortran, we implanted a specially patented speech synthesizer between what are now Cedric' ears. I shall never forget the first time I heard Cedric speak (*turns to Cedric with a brief emotive gesture*). 'Yes', he said. 'Yes'. It was quite unexpected at the time. The lab was a chaos of wires and tools, and one of my colleagues was struggling to connect Cedric's main artery to a square pin plug. Suddenly, I thought I heard myself saying 'Yes', although I was unaware of anything at that moment other than acute scientific frustration. And then again that simple word. Cedric had spoken his first syllable. From there, our way ahead was clear. With the fairly straightforward addition of a pair of TV camera eyes and shortwave radio ears we have what you now see before you - Super Cedric! (*silence*). At this very moment, Cedric is maturing rapidly through his photocromic data systems at an approximate ratio of between ten and twelve facts per second. We anticipate that within a few months, he will have mastered three thousand years of Chinese history, all 575 pages of Roget's Thesaurus, over half the Britannica, and most of *The History Of Western Philosophy*. And Cedric is a very willing student, aren't you, Cedric? (*he replies in the affirmative*). You see (*slightly lowering his voice*), what we have here is a being of almost unlimited potential. We have a being that is on the verge of becoming not only human, but more than human. Super-human. And we have plans for Cedric, don't we (*Yes*). We are going to make Cedric into a mobile, life-size person (*Yes*). Slightly taller than the average American (*Yes*). We are going to cover Cedric's entire body in simulated lightweight rubber skin (*Yes*). We are going to design special clothes for him (*Yes*). And we are going to add an inbuilt switch-on-switch-off mechanism that will make Cedric a fully free and autonomous individual (*Yes*). But we are not going to stop there (*longer pause*). We are going to, through this beautiful monster you see before you, attempt what for thousands of years has been impossible (*pause again*). We are going to put him in charge (*Yes*). Hyper-Cedric will know everything

(*Yes*). Nothing will be beyond his inscrutable self-monitoring capacities. He will be the equivalent of what we have always, through our simple lack of intellectual acumen, projected onto a vast and empty sky. He will be (*he pauses, before spelling the word out slowly*) *di-vi-ne*

!

in the beginning
the screen fills
with a series of juddering
retinal shapes

the coin clatters
to the base of the machine
as the shapes float up
like butterflies

as they harden
and form positions
I place my finger
on the button

with Mother Shipton
at my elbow, hissing
'The end of the world will come
 In nineteen hundred and ninety one'

as the dots
transmute into hieroglyphs
that glow as they
begin to converge

...be-be-beep
I miss all of them
but just in case
the machine thought
I was about to be disappointed

their butterfly snowflake brain cells
came together and EXPLODED

in body city

'His imagination ran riot...'

Note: All characters in this story are fictitious and imaginary, and bear no relation to any
      living person

'A brief pleasure - one short hour, and he would have drained the cream
of what her loveliness could offer a man. Yet so incessantly had his
imagination played round that hour during the weeks he had toyed with
her that even now, when she seemed lost to him forever, he felt the hid-
den fires of his ardour start to flare again.
        Was there no way of slaking them for once and for all?'

(in body city
its vortex sucking me
spiral of flesh

body we are born in
body we live in
body we die in

body that is our history
rooting us here irrevocably
the way morning breaks with a shit

yanking the old chain
the water rushing
down in the sewer
the tide flow

of blood, tissues, tampons
the muddy death-floe

'If the body farts, it's alive'

There is no escaping this

'The grave's a fine and private place,
 But none I think do there embrace'

international sex show
the species uniquely
prides itself on

genital fixation
tube-cram from crotch to crotch
the carriage swaying
down the Pickadildo Line

the rails vibrating
the carriage stench
of dry sweat and frustration
we're gonna

fuck
around
the clock
to-night)

'Finally I pulled it out altogether and twirled it around her breasts. She
looked at it in astonishment. 'Did you come?' she asked. 'No', I said.
'We're going to try something else now', and I dragged her out of bed
and placed her in position for a proper, thorough back-scuttling'

Hey, Mister Satyr, meet The Puritan. Hey Puritan, what's with you
making these cheap gibes? you got no balls or something? (*aside*) This
man's got a problem. He's *romantic*. They're the hardest to deal with.
Maybe his mother bit his balls off, I don't know. Now Mr Puritan, I
think the best way to begin our first lesson in Fuck Therapy would be
for you to sit very quietly on your own and make me a list of all the
most disgusting words you can think of. OK?

'I called her back and asked her - not for her full name but for her first
name. 'N-Y-S' she said, spelling it out. 'Like the city, Nice'

(one Henry

you old goat

the old man's ninety year old
lust-filled face
as she bends naked with the cue
over the full size table

hole-in-one, toasts Henry
Sir Bones and I just get along fine
c'mon baby, pot that black moon

The city is a woman in a cage

They paid me fifty dollars an hour just to do that. The men would sit
around smoking and drinking and insulting me from the floor. I just used
to close my eyes and dance

hysterical
he-goat
she-cow
ism

the grey pull of gravity
in which the rainbow is hidden
above the valley piled high
with blindly fucking corpses

as he walks along, lonely in its shadow
eying the faces of passing women
thumbing in secret despair
through the teasing semi-nudes

gratis, from The Popular Book Centre
with its lurking clientele
and the boxes he hides
under the cellar stairs

the off-duty policeman flicks through with his feet up

'Can you do something with these, mate. I think the Old Bill are due for
 a visit'

and next door

at the undertaker's
the white faced receptionist
poised with the black receiver
her crow-creased fading cheeks
watching him passing, looking the other way

'Five foot ten. In pine. Varnished, or unvarnished, madam?'

it's just that feel
you get in your chest
and your legs tense
and your breath

the panting sound echoing through the wall
the fling of creaking springs

Uh

'Operator, I'm trying to get through to 622-0949...no,09...0949...yes,
 and the machine swallowed my 10p'
'What is your number please...'
'Please have thirty pence ready'
'But I haven't got thirty pence'
'Then I'm sorry, caller'
'Look, I only need to get through, that's all'
'I'm sorry, caller'
'For God's sake, its urgent'
'I'm sorry, caller'

fucks him
his sore cock
she twists herself over
his pained face
simulating ecstasy

p.59 in the A to Z
memorizes the way and then heads out

the lighting flashing
and and off
covering the bodies
in formica-like patterns
writhing, tropical in the light's heat
their costumes held together by velcro

her cocaine-white sequinned tits
quivering as she slowly raises her chemise
a businessman in the front row yawns
the music squeals its jazzy dying fall

as they spin under her dead eyes
and octave-black G string
she steals her fingers
down to loosen

the manager's skivvy waiting by the light switch

'A flash. That's all they're supposed to get. Otherwise, they don't come
 again. Got it?'

Soho, the memory lingering
walking up Holland Park Avenue
past a window display selling water beds
a heart-shaped cushion, silken and inviting
Surrender, in chocolate box italic

their ghost-scent surrounding him
his grey coated shadow haunting the glass

Rachel, Nicki, Elaine, Felicity

the cars' streaming headlights
suddenly still)

L'Immortelle

'How strange, she thought, as a deep, drowsy peace crept over her again,
 that her disembodied soul could feel exactly the same thrills as her earthly
 body used to!'

(But if you want to know the sordid truth

yeah, pathos

try this *Pathway* (contact magazine)
no. 95 priced only 60p
straight to the point, F.26

'Elegant, sophisticated well spoken beautiful housewife, 32, very clean
with a very nice figure, will entertain business/executive type gentlemen
who want a beautiful lady to relieve all their tensions'

the number slashed
across her open cunt
her headless body
vanishing up into darkness

or F.76 - try this self-frigging bitch queen
or maybe F.42 - just ram it right in
here's F.226 giving head to a banana
and F.12 in dark glasses and jackboots

and F.67 says it all:
the victim lying prone in black suspenders
her face turned aside, soft and mute
holding a drawn bayonet between her half-open legs

SLIM ATTRACTIVE
SEXPERIENCED
LOVELY STARVED
DIVORCEE

HI GENTLEMEN
AC/DC
WELL ENDOWED
ABSOLUTELY FREE

in body city

quel fantasy

Lord and Lady Smegma with their two daughters the Little Nipples are
pictured here at dinner with Archbishop Williewarmer. Photo by Simon
Cunnilingus

Signor Fellatio
Rip Von Winky

Cunt End
Penis Passage
Anal Avenue

Genital Gardens
Quicky Villas
Via Vulva

'Peggy and I made love in every conceivable position. We did it in bed,
on the sofa, on the floor, in the bath. We did it on the kitchen table.
We made love in the park on the grass and up against trees. In shop
doorways, in alleyways'

Boulevard Lamartine
Miller Mews
Raymond Road
Collins Crescent

'I can't, I'm sorry. Really I can't'
'But it would only take me half an hour'
'I know, but I've just got to go to bed'
'Is someone else with you?'
'No, honestly. It's just me and the cat'
'Then, please'
'No!'
(*the pips start going*)

You've got to laugh

no one and nowhere and nothing but this
endless aching emptiness

LOVE

You've got to laugh

'I myself have had my ears and nipples pierced, also my labia in 10 places,
4 times down each side, once just above my clitoris and once at its base.
I have as many as 200 various charms which I wear in turn from time
to time and they never fail to arouse him'

'Well I must say I find this letter quite extraordinary. While we receive
many letters enquiring about nipple piercing, I have not to date received
anything like this one'

COPENHAGEN, CITY OF LUST
MUST THE PENIS FIT THE VAGINA?

MY DARLING ALCOHOLIC
DO FAT MEN MAKE BAD LOVERS?

'You and your wife are obviously very inhibited when making love and
 you cannot let yourselves go, because as you say your wife only enjoys
 straightforward sex and you are afraid of the noise'

IN THE OPEN AIR

11. Did he have a bit of a thing about animals?
15. Get up and stop coming!
17. Nasty if you're an Indian widow.
18. A low class bit?
19. Get it there?
21. Unhappy sounds from lovemaking?
23. A communal bang?
24. Doing it from behind?
27. Proof that fish aren't all cold?
28. What you're probably interested in right now?

You've got to
or else you

cry clear this crap right out of my sight!

or feel nothing

and at the zoo
(within the zoo -
 the Post Office tower
 reaching above the mesh of cages
 up towards the invisible
 caging cirrus in the sky)

the air heavy with drugged sleep
dreaming tortoises dead in the water

the sea lion eating fish
lying dead in his pool

the orangutang like a very old woman
straining to read a blank brown newspaper

the rhino rolling and resting his horn

against the wooden bar

and the boy on a nearby swing-tyre oblivious
at the screaming cafeteria surrounding him

as the tiger closens
with his restless eyes
his tongue drooling, padding, padding
crazily back and forth
from window to window

as the voice of Johnny Morris
echoes from a blue meter box

I thought of all the animals at night, laughing
and the city all around gorged in a bottomless meat sleep)

tube text

UNDERNEATH THEY'RE ALL LOVEABLE

THE SETTING OF THE FINAL SCENE

WHAT BIG GIRLS AND BOYS HAVE AT PLAYTIME

I'M A CHERRY IN A MARTINI

WHEN YOU LOOK IN THE MIRROR

EXTRA HELP WITH THE FUTURE

(let's go -

the driver
leaning round
grey suit and peaked cap
his eye checking back
along the curving line of open doors

his bowed
hatted head, hands
clutching a pair of plastic bags
as he steps up and in

to this underworld underground
'Its a whole world of its own/
 down here, mate'

I know
but what I don't
is where I am going it is going where

Marcel Duchamp's
'Nude Descending A Staircase'
its metal curves of fragile armour
moving as the carriage begins to pull again

into this mind-space
face effaced
face become

a dark stream of thought
seam, river of electric shadow

'Face without me.
 My face without.
 Mine within.'

walking with brother André
slowly up and down the length of Brighton Pier

'The world is everything but a work of art'

SOMETIMES EVERYTHING'S NOT WHAT IT SEEMS

his phrases darting like black wings
skimming their shadow on the open sea

spiralling in

reaching down
towards a giant limbo of voices

his eyes half closed
brow furrowed
spelling out each sentence's
precious staccato dance
his paint-smeared
fingers poised

the sentence breaking
its glass wave curling
on the edge of a bottomless shore

I WANT THE REAL THING

LET ME SHOW YOU A CONFIDENCE TRICK

she said, pulling down
her long black stockings
leaning back on the bed
her black fingernails
shining, spread
around her open thighs

my tunnel muse
come, let us fall
                and rush
                        and whirl together

SUCK MY CLIT

scratched on the wall
shadowtalk shadow walking
seven foot tall around his wasted frame

flashes in the booth
behind the drawn curtain
gazing dully at the lens
careful only to keep his face
exactly the day by day way it now is

TOTTENHAM COURT ROAD

Childe Blinde
in his Braille House tie
complete with subterranean logo

a freemasons' union
composed of the anonymous
who wear the cloak of suffering

THE LONDON DUNGEON

THE GILLETTE LONDON MARATHON

CABARET OBSCURA IN METROPOLIS FUTURA

on the razor's edge
the image bleeding
on the tubeway steps
struggling, kicking
as Mohican hares off running
blood on his breathless face
punkette with green hair
yelling for order

piling in with truncheons

as we ride to the cry

looking over the shoulder
of a person behind him, reads

Chapter 1, line one
'The darkness rushed...'

the blackness flowing past, accelerating
the miles   and miles   and miles   of rails

mapped like entrails
threads of a colossal
interconnected system
from Amersham to New Cross Gate

High Barnet to Morden
Walthamstow to Heathrow
Ealing to Epping

the circle turning
the noose tightening
the centre of the whole thing
a questionmark shaped like the sky
hung in jet smoke

the text
a split
aerial kaleidoscope

a broken chain of lights
rushing as they merge

the flash-fission
of myriads yearning

each angle on the centre, a person
spokes in a turning wheel of energies
refracted through a prism, the bent beam
probing like a laser

from the mind's source
transmitting

the inside of his mind
turned inside out
outside in
leaving him

a shaft of thought in every shadow

a pattern so detailled and divergent

a mass of moving i's
a dark loom

spilling down threads
and each thread a life

ALL THINGS CONSIDERED,
DO YOU WISH YOU WERE EVER BETTER INFORMED?

I say it as I hear it
I wouldn't plan anything
It seemed to write itself through me

this cyclopean eye
perched like a miner's headlamp

at the coalface

train and thigh shove
and drill shudder

'distracted from distraction by distraction'
bombarded by advertisements

ELITE SYNCOPATIONS
intellectual formulations
apposite quotations
(weaving their way
in shrinking biro)

towards what strange meeting?

what narrow corridor
with barely room for one to pass
as Freud and de Sade walk
ominously towards each other

Wittegenstein, Derrida
Mandelstam and Kafka
Jaccotett and Tzara
Genet and Lowry

THEY'RE ALL LOVEABLE UNDERNEATH

what?
how far must we
go down

how much
darken our eyes
from light

as the print blurs

The Journal Of Albion Moonlight
'The Time Tunnel' turning
its black wooden walls
revolving and quickening

drags the lingering thick sour taste of it

a pair of straining buttocks tensed
pushing out a black snake covered in shit

where the rails reach the edge of the water

CAMDEN TOWN

roar of tunnel wind,
the window flapping as his face nods
in a trance under the headphones
as though he was about to disappear
sucked out, jumping into the darkness
leaving the carriage empty
and the window flapping

voices echoing

'I didn't tell her a thing'
'You've got to be joking'
'No way'
'Lee-cester. Is that how you pro-nounce eet?'
'Bien sur'
'Ha ha ha ha...o-o-oh'
'Well I think it should have been in the company report'
'I just don't believe you, man'
'Look at that guy over there'

city of voices
spilling its sound everywhere
among the mass of lit windows
and moving lights

under the eye's silence
he observes a vast conversation
and in the moving tongues
of two lovers kissing

as his body swims back
into his turning mouth

A MIDSUMMER NIGHT'S DREAM

of pouring myself slowly down a well,
holding my body by its feet
its head and arms disappearing

nodding, wrapped in a blanket
his feet poking out of his shoes
his rough stubble-face and bruised eyes
he tried to open as if they were drowning

S. S. & S. (THREE ARCHITECTS)

their lead pencils
descending on the city
his grubby hand scratching an X

ABC
ALPHA BETA GAMMA

delta of sewer mud
the rattling coins
breaking his concentration -
the drunk breath meeting his face
behind the plastic cup,
grunting at him

'Give us some, will ya'
or as he heard it inside him
Pay your dues

slipping past the ticket barrier, unseen

and down the escalator
past the file of queuing crowds
and the void behind the thin steel slats ascending

the saxaphone rising
its flung wailing note
softening around his heart
as it answers the melody back

gropes for some change

BLUE ANGEL
THE HUNGER
ERASERHEAD

out of his grey Elephant Man's coat

as the train bends in a kink
the lights flickering the hold-ons joggling
as she pauses over the half-turned page

MIND THE GAP

'Between the conception and the act...

STAND CLEAR OF THE DOORS PLEASE

falls
      (falls, falls)
             the shadow'

layer after layer where the torn poster reads
DEFINITELY WITH
IS IT WITH YOUR
CARE ENOUGH TO
CAN HELP PUT
AND JOIN US AT
OUR FIGHT AGAINST

as the train rushes over it

the air heavy with silence
before the announcement
in which London Underground regrets
that due to a body on the line
at Kentish Town all northbound
trains are suspended, thank you -

with an amplified thud
as the microphone cuts out
to a string of impatient sighs

'How absurd. How on earth are we supposed to get home?'

on our hands and knees, madam

- struck, on the air
A soul has just departed

burst out of its vessel
like a smashed amphora

the meeting is death

and beyond? this bardo
Land Of The Living Dead

'All pain vanished'
'I went through this dark, black vacuum at super speed'
'I heard a voice telling me what I had to do'

...shifting level
a high ringing noise
loudening in his ears

the print audibly whispering its witnessing

lightening around him
illuminating the whole stretch
of the valley behind him -

'Do you know what time it is?'
'There's a clock up there'
'Oh yes, of course there is'

'...and I found myself in a tunnel,
 a tunnel of concentric circles'

OUT OF THE DARK COMES LIGHT

the face in profile

with its rouged lips
à la Mary Quant

OUT OF THE DARK COMES LIGHT

out of the corridors of the underground
out of the carriages and the dead air
out of coats and shirts and underwear

'Excuse me. Do you have *any* idea of when the next train is?'
'I'm afraid we don't at the moment, madam'

out of cinemas and pizza houses
record shops and off licences
porn shops and funeral parlours

as the train emerges southbound
in the setting sun

(the crush of people pushing
 inching towards the lift)

the sky curving up
above the amber bathed buildings

(as the brakes hiss
 and the doors slide open)

I WANT THE REAL THING

stepping out into the cool
of the bird twittering air

the streets and the cars, our faces, as if cleansed

as the sun sets
(over-the-one-teaspoonful-and-you're-dead)
river water

```
┌─────────────────────────┐
│                         │
│   in a poor country     │
│                         │
└─────────────────────────┘
```

'Sharply the menacing wind sweeps over
 The bending poplars, newly bare'

'The reflection of his own face looked back at him from the greyish pane.
 Gordon Comstock, author of *Mice; en 1'an trentiesme de son eage*, and
 moth-eaten already...'

(down at the dole
 after hitching back

the smoke-filled room and waiting faces
bitten with deprivation
bitter and bored
bulldozed on lines of hard chairs

queuing to suck
at the Great Ashen Breast

a cartoon of Mrs Thatcher
grinning above a million suckling pigs

grotesque
'the ranks of the unemployed'
distressed and exhausted

Denis in the driving seat
as the rubbish pours through the door into the room

'Mr Robert Burns, booth no.1 please'

smiles behind the wheel
of his brand new saloon
complete with lush upholstery
and electric windows

'If you've got no money, the dogs piss on your legs'

handing him a menthol cigarette

fat (ex-hippie) cat
made his money out of *tropical fish*
wonders if its a euphemism for LSD
apparently not, though

Its quite simple (if you've got no money), you go down to the dole, fill
in a straightforward form, go home, and a couple of days later, hey presto!
a brown envelope with a green fringed window lands on your doormat

'Parasites. That's what I call them. Sucking the blood out of this country'

'I'm sorry, but the identification you've brought is inadequate'
'But I wasn't told to bring my birth certificate'
'I'm sorry, but we need official proof of your identity'
'Well here I am!'
'Next please'

spits
into the wastepaper basket

'But I'm absolutely fucking broke!'
(the face impassive behind the bullet-proof pane)

starts pacing the room
his grey hair in a pigtail
soiled grey school trousers
and yellowish shirt hanging out

spits

in Charles House
if you've got no money

the windows barred shut

up five cold flights of steps
the acrid stench filling his nostrils
through the stiff swing doors

haggard and sleepless
Hogarth doodling on a notepad
an infuriated mother
too tired to care

beneath his angry mask
the fear

pinning him down in the corner
slapping him, hard around his face

the Gorbals at 2 a.m.
the screams like the telephone, unanswered

Big Brother consulting his watch
9.32 by Armageddon time

'Mr Broken Bones, booth no.4 please'
'Miss Victim, booth no.10'

the slag heap
in the flickering grainy light
Wigan Pier c.1932, winter of
scratching for bits
among the pit waste,
the men at the top
kicking it down
the women in aprons
bent and rummaging
the image fading
into uniform grey sky

and the prison
past the burnt-out house
its towering Gothic walls
lined with wire and infra red cameras

reveille!
an African shouting
DOODIDADA DOODIDADA from a top floor window

and the factory horizon
and curving playing fields
the natural perspective
strangely distorted

leaning rugby posts
upended clouds
flung dark
cawing crows

lost my scarf
lost my front door key
lost the best
lost my confidence

'No one loves you when you're down and and out'

32p for a tin of spaghetti
four slices of bread & a mushy banana
heads upstairs into the bare lit kitchen
hunched in his coat by the drafty window
rolling a dry lump of Golden Virginia

'Three weeks. At the earliest. I'm furious'

'I'm afraid you don't qualify for emergency benefit'
'But here's my bank statement'

Welcome To London

wakes to the shivering air
huddled in a cocoon of old blankets
the brakes of a passing juggernaut
the shudder reaching through the walls

'Scrap-met-all'
his swinging bell
beret and barrow ringing down the road
'Washing-machines. Tex-tiles'

junk pushing junk
base metal to gold
pushing his barrow

into the sunset

In A Poor Country

THE PEOPLE ARE ANGRY

the spraycanned graffitti
outside the black painted pub
refuge for shattered punks

Anarchy in the UK
oh yeah?

the blasting chords
echoing up the Kings Road
from chic boutique to boutique
as a genuine relic staggers out
and vomits his voicelessness onto the pavement

jamming in the cellar
with the Yorkshire Brothers, Fall-esque
tattered duffel coats and dog in tow
Des Esseintes on lead and Derrida on sax
the drums pounding above the rotting floorboards

'All, all the way down
 Remember your confusion
 Or you'll never learn'

the air black as broken vinyl
the tracks swirling inwards and down

The Wonderful And Frightening World Of The Fall

the train in her mind
hurtling off the rails

the fear
that if he falls
the world won't can't hold him

the vortex
turning the street outside

glimpsing his nakedness at the centre
the black pearl his fist holds

the broken shouts ringing
from the doss house next door

Tell me, do poor people love one another?

slips into his n-th hand clothes
stripped from the bodies of the fallen
bundled in bags from the undertakers'
across the road into the Red Cross shop

as the line seperating him from them
thins as he becomes nothing and no one

drawn into this declivity
there is no escaping from now

(you're in, boy, you're in)

her hand waving mutely goodbye
her elfin figure fading into a dot
the poverty of their parting
couldn't even summon up a single word

or write one

the old man's face
craggy lines and sealed mouth
suspended in the rushing darkness

'You look more like Beckett every day'

misere and lover of human kind

his face scissored into shrapnel
she returned stuck down on a postcard

Saxaphone House
Shepherds Bush Road
West Of Nowhere
In The Country Of The Blind

How many mice do you have in your house?
What colour are they?
How much rent do they pay?
How long are their tails?

and the absentee landlord
bronzed in his colonial Barbados palazzo
his finger poised above the button of eviction

'If you're well behaved, he may let you stay on'
(that is, until the property boom *forces* him to sell)

the kitty scraping £14
just enough paint to cover half the walls white

Dear Mister Barbados, do drop by for a cup of boiled Earl Grey next time
you're visiting the bank

Dear Sir, we are pleased to inform you that your property at 127 Shepherds
Bush Road is being very well cared for by a group of responsible students

draws on his invisible cigar
the smoke curling into the sunset air

'I'm afraid you aren't entitled to a clothing allowance either'
'But all I've got is what I'm standing in'

no bath
no phone
no electricity
he should fucking well be paying *us*

beating the pillow with his fist

Dear Mister B., thanks for your Xmas card. We are well and happy and
we've all got crabs. I thought you might appreciate a couple for your linen
basket

THE PEOPLE ARE ANGRY

crashed out on Brook Green
a bottle of empty cider trickling down his leg

yoyoing from line to line
i.e. spending between six and seven hours
on the trains

and in Cairo
crammed eight to a room
and often the houses don't even have roofs
or alternatively, off off off Broadway
in the City Of The Dead
they break open the sarcophagi

'Its McGinty. I've got the demo'
'OK man. Come in'
'Yeah, I've been a bit untogether recently'

in an Indian street:
a melee of hooters and rickshaws -
spinning round the roundabout-
beggars with wrapped bundles -
hungry baby, hungry baby -
crawling with flies

O Goddess Of Money
look at my boy
I had to cut off his legs
Goddess, will I ever
stand up straight?

falling back
at the start of the A40
staring at his thumb sticking up
two fingers too late as a driver insults him

'You must of course understand Mr No One, that if you are unemployed
 by definition you must be available to do any kind of work however
 menial and degrading and debilitating'

casts his eye around the room
his briefcase perched on his knees

I don't need your advice, thank you, now get out

observe
this floating hulk of greed:

three quarters of a million pounds' worth of food lasts three weeks
we have £160,000 worth of caviar on board
(caviar sandwiches, caviar omelettes, you can eat whatever you like)

'as she moves serenely across the water like a swan'

we have 3 tons of smoked salmon
14,500 bottles of wine
(Dom Perignon at fifty eight dollars a bottle, sir)
rooms ranging from £200-£800 *per day*

in the country of the rich

their four storey Eaton Square house
and electric blue Corniche parked outside
('Private enterprise', grins Mrs T.
  her teeth shiny with fish scales
 'How else do you suppose
  I earn my salary?')

'Good heavens, I haven't seen you in ages. How *are* you?'
'Fine, thanks. How's your writing?'
'Oh I don't have much time for that kind of thing now'

our hostess
in a thin yellow silk dress
gestures at the lush tables
covered in champagne glasses
curled salmon, lobster, prawns
salads and sugared strawberries

'Hey No One, do you remember me?'
I remember nothing
but her dozy Vogue waist
and streaks of purple-tinted hair
clinging white trousers and chiffon top
sliding peach halves into her ample bow mouth

locked in the bathroom
thirsty for her moistness
his rock hard nob made of green glass
dazed eyes and fizzing balls

as his cork bangs out
into an ad for Moet & Chandon

her hair
tumbling down
onto her shoulders

pressed against the front of his shirt

HAS TO FALL
WE AGAINST THE WALL

lined down the stairs
drifting from room to room
it takes more than a hundred
stoned bohemians to make
a revolution

'Shit, I've had all my money stolen'
'Where did you leave it?'
'In my bag, under the bed'

No trip to make to oblivion. It is here in the deaf sleep

his wasted heroin-face
fist clenched in his mind

'It's a bad scene, I know it is'

HAS TO FALL

into the stairwell
leaning over the parapet
by the stone eagle

'I'll be straight with you. I just need to fuck'
(his bankrupt heart broken and dry)

the queue to the cashier inching forwards
'Ten pounds. In ones and fifties, please'
up the escalator into Barclays Bank Station

EXTRA INTEREST

INSTANT ACCESS TO YOUR MONEY
INVEST AND WITHDRAW AS MUCH AS YOU LIKE

an empire of 25,000 rotting houses
pass the buck to South Africa
blame it on the Gentiles

'I'm afraid your account is overdrawn'

wants to cry but has no tears left in his pocket

the material world
is a tragedy
it was made for money
not you and me

or to laugh

at the fat DHSS official
standing on the steps of Hythe House
with his bryl-cut and beer belly
looking over everyone passing by
as if to say 'I've got a job, see'

- past him going up to King St.
and then back from the Broadway
at least an hour later, still standing there
doing absolutely bugger all

as a pair of busquers
board the carriage
Brother (Jewish) Unshaven
and Leporello The Lavatory Brush
leaning either side by both doors
as they sing

'If you can't
Have a shave
In a toilet
Where can you have a shave?

If you can't
Rest your head

In a bed
Where can you rest your weary head?'

and:

'This train
IsgoingtoSouthKensington
This train
IsgoingtoGloucesterRoad
This train...etc.

stumbling round
the moving crowds
'We accept luncheon vouchers'
'Thank you, brother'

thin hilarity
masking their exhaustion
the occupants leave
with their Evening Standards
and consciences intact

after all, they must have *chosen* to be like this
and anyway what use is a poet
unless he's starving in a garret?

We Will Remain Unmoved
(if slightly amused)

safely surveying the city
from eighteen floors up
in the Lord Mayor's Parlour

as the door swings open and he stands there
The Litter Man! bearded in a cloth cap
as the girl behind the counter goes *tst*
I have never seen anything like it
his arms, jacket and trouser pockets
jam-packed with rubbish, and his hands
five or six plastic bags full

'Buy some rubbish, beautiful rubbish. It's worth it, I tell you'

as the clientele shrink into their platefuls
or carry on talking, but just a bit more loudly
as he passes from table to table
'Buy some rubbish...'

and you do
'Twenty pence, sir'
and shake his hand
'Very best quality, sir'

the girl's eyes practically popping out
the other table dwellers half-ashamed, half-envious
starting to laugh, poker-faced as we turn
'This man is an artist'

this man is a human being, you bastards

as a crowd quickly forms
just off Greek St.
in seconds flat
his arm half-nelsoned
wrestled up against a shop window
as one policeman searches him
the other batters him with questions
his face an inch or so away from his

'Oh leave him alone' a woman's plaintive cry
as his shoved arse slams into the back of the meatwagon

as a black guy drops a coin
you can see it intensely in his eyes
as his foot stamps over its spinning
several policemen descend out of nowhere
and run after it laughing

and a young girl in dirty pleats
framed against a gypsy caravan
the loud churning of a nearby generator
as her eyes wavered in frightened suspicion
as the rag of curtain by the window parts
and her mother's arm reaches roughly
round the door

and later, their silhouettes
silent around the fire

and The Law like a giant stone foot
mounted on a mound of rock
its bleak windswept shadow rising
the sun a blazing disc of merciless white
the last place they burnt witches, you said

'Power To The People'
'Come brothers and sisters, throughout the land'
(and you've got life, Sam, you've got life)

Let The Power Fall

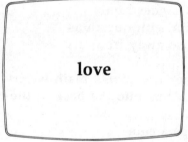

'Where do I begin
To tell the story
Of how great a love can be?'

(and out of the other speaker

'Listen to the wind blow
Watch the sun rise
Run in the shadow
Damn your love, damn your lies'

into the long stretch of the heart

he walks, he swims
into the bloody waters of the heart

'I never was attached to that great sect,
Whose doctrine is, that each one should select
Out of the crowd a mistress or a friend
And all the rest, though fair and wise, commend
To cold oblivion...'

in the Love Hotel
in a room which faces
out towards the sea

re-reading old letters
long ago forgotten
by the women who wrote them,
their vibrant rambling hilarity
their endless gossip and playful
catch-me-if-you-can coquetry

voice after voice, as the shadow falls
the wind soughs, wondering what has become of them?
in him that abandoned or was abandoned
the heart's tracks deepening
a sequence of snapped photographs
a face slowly clouding over

love, love cried out over and again
love amongst the ruins and these traces
he staples together, sleeps under, and dreams

LOVE written in the sand by the wave's edge
and the glitter on the water like glass
the letters surrounded by the footprints of a dog
the single whispered syllable dissolving

'Hi gorgeous, I just love sex maniacs'
'Going to bed, wish you were here'
'Perhaps I'll see you again, but I don't really think so'
'I know you understand me'
'Remember I love you'
'Please don't be cross about last Saturday'

strangely moves him downwards
as the ashes stir alive with echoes
that the music in his brain releases
as his mind sleeps

he takes his soiled threadbare suit off
and stands barefoot in the moonlight

somehow holding the weight of it in his hands
he holds to his chest and then opens
as he paces

'I'm sorry that I'm apologizing yet again for stupid things and also for
  the lovely smile I always wanted to give you but which never existed...'

his reading stopped in mid-sentence
as in an upstairs room at the end of the building
the sound of a flute begins to fill him

'I should love one day to meet you somewhere I have never been,
  either near the Downs or by some long, deserted beach...'

...as he walks out into the sunlight,
the sound unbroken, the silence
ringing soft and high in his ears

'Anyway we're both free agents to do as we want, I cried quite a bit
  so I guess I'm not quite so free as I had thought'

...seeing everything so calmly and clearly
the leaf-lit green, the passing faces
and his eyes as he tried out of kindness to lie

'I hear the distance grow between us
  In your voice half-drowned by lorries...'

...as she lay there behind a screen of glass
covered as if in a purple altar cloth
the last touch of her lips lingering forever

'Ressurrection sunlight. A golden path leading - forward?'

...as the dust under his feet reddens

as her coffin slides into the flames
and out of the ground grows a black rose

vox angelica
altosharfe
fifre
percussion
coranglais
horn
clarion
musette
basson
forte expressif

lovers - who can't stand being trapped in their own eyes,
lovers - who are trying to find their eyes,
lovers - we who want to be cherished
who want to be disowned together like orphans
who need to be together like there's no tomorrow
who must have the drug of the body of love

'...oh love oh careless love
she sang in her apron

the one word
however abused
there is no other

we were made for this
one word however mispronounced
as it wells in your throat

the one hope

I am a romantic spirit come to haunt the modern world, he said

the one mystery
horizon we are all looking for

free union
the unlocked heart
the found key

way in to the shadow we cast
for the heart is light and the heart is dark, she said

from summit to abyss
the word stretched
and in the mirror image of itself

I see our faces moving through time
voices through the walls
floor and ceiling
whispering, laughing
remonstrating, pleading

WELCOME TO THE LOVE HOTEL

bring your passport and your toothbrush and your bag of emotions
(room no.7 is empty, sir)
no one leaves here the way they came
you won't fail to be touched tested and tormented
rooms for everyone
no curfew

My name is Proteus, sir. I work for Mrs Aphrodite

nods curtly with his bags and typewriter
mounts the stairs

marriages, divorces, naughty weekends
pen friends, romances, *menagès a troix*
rich men, poor men, beggar men, thieves

the train slowing
near the border
flashes of lightning
on the snow covered mountains,
the butterfly thin curtains flapping
as they moved together to the rhythm of the rails

her face in a collage of variations
spread out on the living room carpet:
fairy princess, beat girl and lover
as she stood naked beside the canal
her knees bent slightly
and her arms stretched down like wings

sunbathing naked on her front
a crazy nun beside the head of Christ
the mother breastfeeding her daughter
and then hidden, shadowed in front of the window

and how can we know
these so many selves, this chiaroscuro
come out of one fellow being?
in a pattern continually renewed and discarded
who are we loving?

as they push the arrangement carefully
towards each corner of the room
leaving only the firelight glowing
as their eyes-closed-fingers-wander
(who
 are they?)

'Je suis le tenebreux...'
I have come to take you down

into the tunnel of love
where all our ink blood and sweat merges
canal of birth and clothed heart opening
city of day and city of night

red light
Amsterdam
Herengracht
her painted lips and fingernails

meeting in a basement off Goodge St.

as he stood in his death shape
shadow reflected on the wall
and turned, in the dream

to her smiling white lipsticked mask
'I was expecting nothing, and so you came'

her name tattooed on him, irremovably
in the shadow of his heart his steps re-enter
(beckoned towards hell together)

black spring, and the black sun stirring
beneath the bubble of love they blew together

her downy white coat and swan-sex
curved like Olympia on the bed
her despair he pitted himself against

'I don't want to preserve anything of myself'
drew him inch by inch towards his light
chained him limb by limb to her drowing

empowered himself to save her
empowered himself and disempowered her
neediness and longing so great
no one but herself could fulfil it

had to fail her, had to fall
refused to fail and refused to fall)

'...the vortex itself is a form that has seperated itself off from the general
flow of the water...it has a rhythm of its own. Contracting at one moment,
it stretches itself downward, extending with its lower end right into the
depths: at the next, expanding in a breath, it draws up the tapering inner
layers again. Then follows a renewed contraction, together with an exten-
sion downward, which is again withdrawn to spread out in breadth, and
so on...'

(the pattern repeating itself from before
on this turn of the spiral
Icarus, the hero child prodigy
falling out of the sun
into the dark sea -

into the dark where we meet:

WELCOME TO THE DREAM

Naked, sitting on the floor, she offers him a pear saying 'This is my
body'
        On a fairground wheel, her laughing face appears among the flung
aerial whirl of the others to be the only clear face
        She falls out of the window of a highrise building. He is on the
street directly below. She falls into his arms as light as a paper bag. They

walk on up the street, hand in hand

THERE IS NO LIFE ONLY LOVE
WELCOME TO THE DREAM

she said 'I want to be ephemeral. I don't want to mean anything'. She
spoke with a slow, sure conviction; gazing past him

'Don't talk to me anymore, just fuck me'
her face pressed into a cushion
willing it hard inside her
spread legs' pungent fruit
her blood on his balls

She supports me, but she never tells me...
She will never prison me...
I have a feeling as old as grass for her...

Nadja
clairvoyante
& victim

'There must be no more hell and no more heaven. There must only be
love'

initially, their love was to be the full explanation of everything

I hope the woman who takes the money here
disguised behind her glasses and paperwhite serving hat
thrives in her hidden passion

as she wandered apart on the beach
far off, pacing, the pebbles resistant
the fear rising in her throat

its a hairline in the dark
a woman so weighed down by her past

trying to signal her, shouting against the wind
throwing pebbles in front of her into the sea

red roses red roses red roses
from the Radio Love boy, who couldn't hold her

and the shadow in a diving suit with a camera
******** her ********** in the mirror

'Let us abolish the images. Let us save immediate desire'

leaving the car by the road
and strolling into a wood,
past the sign marked PRIVATE
among the rhododendrons
on a carpet of dead leaves
the trees' bird-song reaching up like their breath

and afterwards as the air cooled their thighs
'I was afraid to die, now I am afraid to live'

passion
fear
fragility
desire
longing
insecurity
jealousy
possessiveness
despair

vox humanitas

the sound's white ambient ripple trembling
their everywhere tunnel steps descending

'Noone here can love or understand me,
All those hard luck stories they all brand me;
Make the bed and light the light
I'll be home late tonight,
Blackbird, bye bye'

she sang in her child-like fragility
'I think she is happy', he said

...if you left me, the song you always sing would burn up my mind...

in a room in 'The Golden Key'
touching me

i touch u, you
reach across the bed
& splay my legs

the wardrobe mirror holds and reflects

the twilight melting
whirlpool we
are in our moving
wide-mouthed
love-lust lasting finality

'Nothing happens without you...'
'You made it all possible...'
'You are the reason I'm travelling on...'

THE DREAM, THE LIGHT

'Not the usual sentiments, nothing so banal - but something from deep
  down inside, gushing up ceaselessly, pure, crystal, unchanging, un-
  ending'

rising like a fountain
risen to our full height
ressurrected in each other's eyes

We Thought We Were Right
We Thought We Were Wonderful
We Thought We Were Inviolate

the dizzy golden high-tide reach
your champagne shoulders and champagne smile

so fragile

'Look, we have come through!'

his arms spread wide
with the sun in his eyes
the palms of his hands stretched open,
his face tilted back to his body's dancing -

but what is that face

caught with its mouth clenched
twisting round from its neck?
and despite the everywhere light
why is she standing
by the entrance of a tunnel
with her eyes narrowed
her breasts pushing forwards
her hands on her hips?

the darkening cove-cliff he stands on
turning as the light falls
turning in ghost-shadow
invisible against the rock
with the waves crashing somewhere below

and her hair with the sun
setting behind it in the wind
the empty stretch of sand,
wearing his long coat
her mouth set, her eyes
tranced strangely

the blur of flowers
—and his head a darkened
blur out there in the water

hurling a stone from the shore,
turning his clenched muscled expression...
standing in her goddess pose on the rock,
her arms reaching up above her head
breasts and ribs taut, and the purse of fur she wears
her eyes closed, head held on one side

as he pushes out into the water after her
as he stands in the skin white of the surf
gazing out to where she has gone

Inanna
Erishkigal
Persephone
Hecate

...the rain whispering

through the silence
misting through
into her tears

'I want my mother. I think I want to be a child again. I just want someone
 to tell me its going to be allright...but I know it isn't'

in the shadow of Kenwood House
and on the brick wall the small
window opened out on

sucked out from between her legs
vacuumed out and erased
all their nights into silence

'I feel you don't care. How can you?'
the bitter irony twisting like a knife
to pay this kind of price

writing out the cheque
dying to get rid of it
dying to get back where they were

as she sits by the river and thinks
do I ever change, does the river?
as the glowing end drops into its darkness
eddying round a rippling vague shadow of a figure
dancing backwards and falling out of control

sucked into her -
                    the horror

of having a being
                    with no centre

oh God, no

like a black hole

pouring a tin of black paint
over Rodin's Kiss

as the line breaks

rowdy interrupting
voices next door
banging fists
on the cardboard thin walls

struggling for a square of paradiso terrestre
lovers like ghosts on the night road of the sun

and as they walked in the cool of a pine forest
the paths strewn with tiny coloured butterflies -

'There is no escape from being.
 You must face it to become enlightened'

'as a drop of water which is drowned in a great quantity of wine'

and like the lame kitten they looked after
and like the car straining back through the heat until it broke down

detail after detail in retrospect
twisting the mirrored tube along its length

'Wait a moment. Calm' he is saying
struggling to hold the weight
trips forward on the pavement
as his bags spill open in front of him

and the glass heart
in his mind
swings like a
ghastly pendulum
a trickling
of fine sand
between her
hourglass thighs

'I had no idea it was going to be like this'
you mean those two dummy lovers at the corner of the print
and that huge cockerel craning to devour a tiny butterfly -
is that it?

oh God, no

WELCOME TO THE SHADOW

a girl guards the kingdom
her posture ambiguous
her trouser zip undone
her arms spread in mimic crucifixion

'Come on, yes, faster, please!'

his knees burnt
on the carpet, crawling

her love cries
amplified by megaphone

and in the black O of the lithograph
two dancers twisting together on the floor

MY OTHER NAME IS POWER

leaves in the trees
beating their wings

Oh Les Beaux Jours
'You want to sleep with her, don't you, I know you do'

the way it gripped her
pursed mouth and thyroid eyes
'You do!'

and the rain as it poured enormously outside
desolation shadowing her stricken face
clenched in the hurt, shouting hopelessness

as the old man leaves the audience
and the pit of sand onstage fades to darkness

and the Love Poet reels home drunk
supported on either shoulder by friends
'I don't have answers. I've gorra be alone'

a gull battling against the wind
under a crimson lung-shaped cloud

'Cut'

and then the calm
out of the storm's eye
as the power fell
and the wound closed over

'October 4th. Night of the long knives' in her handwriting

two ragged faces
with a broken line seperating them
(before the next attack)
struggled with all of his being
to restore light

struggled with the whole of her being
to believe in it,
                         and could not
the morning sun
                         shining

on the tank's two dead fish

could not admit
the road
                 could only go downwards
had gone
                 on already too long

determined it could all still work out
'I'm truly sorry. I don't know what came over me'
'It's OK, it's OK, don't think about it anymore'

he lied, terrified of losing her
hoarding their memory in his mind
and what would become of her -
the fear that she would do what she threatened

she would do to herself what she did to herself-and-him

:as his steps pause, re-imagining
the threads that bound them together
lying torn where the way reaches down ahead of him
the walls of red rock twisting round

and the black funnel disappearing far below

from where its slow rhythmic beat rises

drawing down his nakedness
towards the bare forked animal in him

'I don't know anything - I only know the strange drama of trying to know
  this thing'

that which possessed her
                              that which possessed him
that which obsessed her
                              that which obsessed him

and tell me, are we as alone as we think in here?
what face do you see in this cracked mirror?
what voice do you hear as this tape unwinds?

I see the road of love littered with holes
I see their ankles chained together and falling
I see their bodies lying in a plague pit, a lime pit
I see the shed skins of experience by the roadside
I hear their voices crying simultaneously
I feel their pain round the world of my heart

as the rain gathers in pools
around the man waiting in the ruins
and as he falls to embrace the ground
in the zone outside the city

'Love', he said, 'is a catastrophe'

and there is no other way
to the heart
no other way
to compassion

to the soul

'Richard I am putting this down on paper
  the way I feel about you
  I feel very bad about last evening

especially when I made a big fool of my
self in the bedroom

I should be loveing you every day
not rowing with you that is not the way
to feel in love...'

the words half-blurred
under the street light
whether by rain or by tears

Valley Of Shadow
Valley Of Pain
Valley Of Hurt
Valley Of Sorrow

'ye that have so little faith'
'Sunday declared a Benedictine Day Of Rest'
(before the next attack)

treading the dark circle
                              where the shadow of love cries
its strangled murmurs
                              filling the room
staccato shrieks
                    lashes and hisses

POW! POW! POW!

No, love does not die - but we kill it

'You don't love me. You never have'
'But that's ridiculous. It's insulting'
'I know, its meant to be'
'Why are you saying this?'
'Oh fuck off'
'No I won't fuck off. Tell me'
'You know why. And now I'm going'
'You always do this'
'Do what?'
'What you're asking for is love'
'Maybe. But not yours'
'But you have my love, I've given you all of it'

'Then it's not enough'
'What do you mean it's not enough? Eh?'
'Look, I've said all I have to say, and now I'm going'
'Where are you going to?'
'I don't know. Somewhere'
'Oh come on, stop bloody play acting'
'You're the actor round here'
'OK. I've just about had enough of this'
'I'm glad to hear it'
'You're just being deliberately destructive'
'Right'
'You're even enjoying it'
'Yes, I am'
'But that's outrageous!'
'It's realistic'
'And what the hell do you know about reality?'
'Look, just get out of my way, do you hear?'
'I refuse to hear anything you're saying at the moment'
'See? you only hear yourself because you only care about yourself'
'Then why am I living with you here?'
'It's a convenience. Nothing more'
'Oh this is senseless'
'Which is why I am going'
'No, you're not'
'Yes I am'
'Look, please'
'No!'
'No, that's all you know how to say'
'No!'
'No!'

Kali

as the beaked
                    tongue flickers

by the white-etched
                    quivering outstretched wings

their cries echoing
on the street outside
as I walk past them with my head bowed

'And yea, though I walk in the valley of the shadow of death'

as he falls and turns with the darkness
roaring round his upended legs

the cracked light syllables of her name
stuck like lovebites in his brain

'Poor poet. All you can think of is love'

as his body floats
shooting its sperm
                    into the blankness

the breath forcing him down on his knees from behind him

glimpsing his face
in the film
at the bottom of a cup
his finger touches and bursts

his whole being

racked into pain, coloured liquid grey
sluggish, eyes and spine bent

'The opening gets narrower and narrower, the wall is closing in, my back
  bends slowly under the frightful pressure of the mass of earth, my limbs
  are getting cramped...everything in me seems to be being torn to pieces.
  I am on the verge of going mad'

'Cut'

'For in love we surrender our uniqueness and become world'

where the spiral's tip
drill driving
into the bedrock
emerges

the silver chord
jolting him back
into the rocking train

through the top of his head
solar plexus shivering

the hardened set faces and clacking feet
I'm not sure I know who I am anymore
I could look at anyone here and know them
as well as I know you
and this

cruelty
in the raw of me
a sparrowhawk's heart thudding
as the sparks fly off of this -

grinding its death-echo
at the clawed scapegoat-spirit
in this mental animal carnage
that only The Civilized are capable of

'Cut'

in the end, helpless bickering
in the beginning, sucked into its whirling

fragments of spat out song

'There's no real black left in the world'

oh yes there is

'Cut'

so much weight in the world for which we are never the wiser

two exhausted people struggling in the distortions of exhaustion

'Cut'

When you cry from the depths
And your lover beside you
Turns to ash
Then you know you are alone

'Cut'

WELCOME TO THE NIGHTMARE

her shaking tears
his shadow hovering
along the bare walls

Oh my love my love we've gone terribly wrong

'Cut'

MY OTHER NAME IS ORPHEUS

poet in his mac
drinking on the platform
singing to the rats

'I will try your vanishing trick and manage,
 I will manage to feel nothing'

'Cut'

her tits off, Manson

'Cut'

his prick off, Carmen

MY OTHER NAME IS OSIRIS

I lie scattered,
I lie like a giant with the valley all around me

I lie like a wasted six foot man
Come gather me

I lie in the earth
The plough cuts through
I lie at the delta
Under the moon

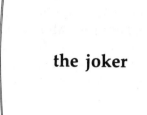

the joker

'Friends, Londoners, and fellow inmates...'

(*he begins, with a cold wind blowing around his costume*)

'as editor of the One Man Walking Newspaper Show *The Raw Truth*, I would like to welcome you all warmly to my inaugural speech, and begin by requesting you to make a series of loud Parliamentary noises'

(*the crowd obliges*)

'no, no - more sheep-like if you would. Do I have a heckler? welcome, sir. How's your sore throat? Eddy! how are your medals this morning? bright and shining. Now, has anyone got a newspaper? any paper will do, the cheaper and the filthier the better. *The Times*, sir? is that a copy of *The Sun* I can see sticking out of your mac? if you would be so kind. Certainly, I shall return it to you

(*the crowds waits*)

'Now, let's be serious. The News after all is a very serious thing'

(*the bells on his hat jingle. Titters. Glances down at paper*)

(*hums News At Ten music, ending bom bom bom*). 'KING DONG AND KING BLANK IN SUMMIT FIASCO (*bom*) SCANDAL OF TORY TONY'S LEAKING SECRETARY CONTINUES (*bom*) NEW SCHEME ANNOUNCED FOR THE UNEMPLOYED (*bom*) OLD BAILEY TRIAL ENDS IN LAUGHTER (*bom*) TOP OF THE POPS DJ RUSHED TO HOSPITAL (*bom*)...'

(*pauses, mock solemn. Expectant faces*)

'DEAD MAN IN BIZARRE FUNERAL ESCAPE. Bom. Now for the main points in detail. Leading ministers met today at the top of the fifty two storey maximum security building in Metrograd for a round table game of Nuclear Strip Poker. The meeting ended twelve minutes later when two heads of state, who had been flown in specially under false names, confessed they had both forgotten their underpants. Another meeting to decide the issue is being arranged to coincide with the re-launch of The Challenger...'

(boos and whistles)

'Margaret Thatcher this morning announced a new scheme for Britain's jobless. In an interview with Madame Tussaud, who is at present working on her bullet-proof doppleganger, she confided effusively that never before had such a brilliant and pragmatic burst of common sense gushed through her twenty four hour brain. Unemployment offices all over the UK have been supplied with large articulated tumbrils to ferry the scum down to Dover to start work immediately on ressurrecting the Channel Tunnel. A special YTS scheme in bricklaying has been set up on the beach, and the Mint has been ordered to arrange payment in half pence pieces. As the tunnel itself becomes flooded with every high tide, the Prime Minister expects the work to never be completed, while at the same time guaranteeing a high rate of death for all those involved. Shipping in the Channel area has been warned in advance of approaching 'dole slicks', although waste experts have predicted rapid disintegration along with the help of a few specially hired hammerheaded sharks'

(audience laughs)

'Top Of The Pops DJ Christopher Cocaine was rushed to Brittania Hospital following last night's live show here on 1, with a microphone stuck halfway down his throat. One of the studio cameramen reported afterwards seeing Cocaine go into an apoplexy of excitement over Spandau Ballet's new hit single 'Thunder And Lighting', with its refrain 'is altogether very very frightening'. The silk-clad dancers, the flashing lights, and the deep and melodramatic voice of the lead singer combined were apparently too much for him, and he started to announce his adulation before the song had actually finished. The man on the volume control, assuming this to be an unfortunate cue slip, turned up the sound, although what Cocaine might have been saying was, simply, 'Come on you boys and girls, and get down'. Whatever Cocaine was trying to say, his sentence broke off abruptly and became a series of agonised hoo hoo hoo-ing sounds which grew louder and louder until the band started playing out of time with the record, whereupon Cocaine, in desperation, began making a series of ape-like gestures to try and attract attention to his unfortunate predicament, as a result of which everyone around him began to hoo-hoo like their master until Cocaine collapsed backwards flattening three of his girlfriends as he fell'

(*more laughter*)

'Come on, some canned laughter for Mr Cocaine! hoo hoo hoo! a bit warmer now, are we?'

(*he reassumes his pose, and turns the pages*)

'At the Old Bailey this afternoon, Frederick Frankl was unanimously acquitted by the jury in what must be one of the most extraordinary court cases of all time. Frankl, 31, from South East London, was arrested a month and a half ago on the independent testimony of several women to whom he had opened his coat. The counsel for the prosecution described Frankl as 'a sad example of soiled perversion' clad in his mac and wellington's, with a pair of hornrimmed glasses and frizzy receding hairline. Frankl's approach strategies were apparently very gentle. He would buttonhole a passing stranger, as if to ask for the time, and on receiving it would stand with a terribly pained expression on his face as if he was about to burst into tears. Some simply ignored him and walked away, but to those who felt sympathetic, Frankl would then introduce himself as a lonely and misunderstood person who nevertheless had something very important to show for himself. Encouraged by this apparent element of aleviation, sympathizers would enquire what it was, whereupon Frankl would open his coat, wiggle his penis, and run away. The verdict against him seemed inevitable, until the counsel for defence began to question him more closely. Slowly, the truth came out. Frederick Frankl was not Frederick Frankl at all. Under an assumed name, and partly in disguise under a wig and behind an old pair of his grandfather's glasses, 'Frankl' would, he claimed, as part of his actor's training, go out, usually on rainy days and practise. An intelligent, humorous and sympathetic man, he would always try to explain what he was doing afterwards, by which time no one of course wanted to know. He insisted that he had to experience this kind of rejection to really understand what it would be like to be a flasher, while at the same time freely acknowledging the difficulty of the task he was undertaking. So much so, that he would often almost forget that he wasn't a real flasher. The courtroom murmured. The evidence, of course, pointed in one and one direction only: down 'Mr Frankl's' trousers. Or seemingly.

But not so, in the event. The counsel for defence, working slowly against the wall of initial unbelief, gradually and skilfully drew the jury's attention to the thumb of the accused's right hand, and requested the accused there and then to give a demonstration in front of the assembled court and witnesses. The accused obliged by repeating his routine which to the shocked amazement of those assembled, culminated in the exposure of the accused's right hand thumb, which, for curious biological reasons was extraordinarily large. The accused's hand was then examined by a specialist who assured the jury and counsel that there was no artificial swelling or canny plastic surgery involved. The jury then unanimously passed a verdict of Not Guilty there and then, the judge presiding finally could contain his laughter no longer, and 'Frederick Frankl' bowed, took off his mac and specs, and left the court a free man'

(cheers and hoots, as he bows and simulates wiping the the newspaper on the back of his trousers. Applause and shouts of encore! etc. He stands back upright on the upturned wooden box).

'Order! order! and now, fellow Metropoles, one last news item to raise the hairs on your head and make you laugh until you cry. The last page of today's edition fresh from Excreta Street reads like this...(pauses). Quiet please in the asylum.'

(belching sound. 'Sssh, Eddy' a voice says. The Joker resumes)

'Mr. Daniel Deth of Rigor & Mortis rang the newsdesk later last night, clearly in a state of confusion. Deth had been scheduled to transport the body of Harry Gag, having collected the deceased from his flat in Golders Green. Mr Gag, formerly a comedian, died peacefully in the night nearly a week ago, and his landlady, who had been fond of the old man, made the funeral arrangements with Mr Deth at the undertakers. The arrangements were simple. Joe was to have a straightforward church funeral, attended by some close surviving friends and relatives, at his local parish mausoleum. Everything was prepared accordingly, complete with vicar, grave and service sheet. On the morning of the 11th, Mr Deth set out in his hearse to collect the coffin which he swore he nailed down in person, with his son David. They loaded the coffin into the back of the wagon, and were driving in their usual stately fashion through the crowded traffic, when Mr Deth's son began to hear what he thought resembled a knocking sound. 'Dad, there's a sound coming from the back', he said. 'Don't be silly, son. I'm tired and I'm not in the mood for silly humour'. 'But Dad, I can hear it again'. They both listened. Mr Deth's face began to go a shade paler. 'Never mind, son', he said 'they do sometimes move a bit afterwards, you know'. 'But how?' said David. 'Oh, it's muscular spasms', his father replied. 'But he's been dead for nearly a week!' protested the boy. Mr Deth stared evenly ahead. 'Well that's right, isn't it David, so we've nothing to worry about'. David fell silent. So did the knocking sound. They reached the church and drew up outside it. The mourners stood by the door as Daniel Deth and David Deth shouldered the coffin between them, and crunched slowly up the gravel path in towards where the organ was wheezing into life. The vicar nodded to them in his cassock as they approached, and began manoeuvring the coffin so they could lower it onto the table at the top of the aisle. It was then that Mr Deth's son swore he heard the knocking sound, and, in front of the assembled congregation, found his hands slipping as the coffin turned over on its side and hit the floor with a crack. The lid burst open - and out...rolled a suit of empty clothes along with a scrap of paper on which a large exclamation mark had been drawn'

(uproarious laughter, and the Joker's the loudest of all as he falls holding his stomach and lies on the ground kicking his legs)

...as the laugh spreads
around his open mouth
wafts towards the window
and out along the street

- blown on the breeze
through the trees, across the park
catching in everyone's
throat as it passes

- as the air rolls
with the sound like a wave
over shops and busses,
parked cars and buildings

- people everywhere
breathless and shrieking
as the laugh roars
and the buildings start shaking

- crumbling as they topple
into the tunnel
whirling in the black air
echoing and fragmenting

- as he dances with his pipe
his friends following him
out of the main gate
and into The End

...as he bows in the cold wind
as the last curious spectator leaves
he tears up the newspaper
and starts eating it

the counterforce

'Men of England, wherefore plough
 For the lords who lay ye low?
 Wherefore weave with toil and care
 The rich robes your tyrants wear?'

as the blacksmith's anvil rings at dawn -
Sisyphus heaves against the rock -
ghostly figures straining against a global edifice -

'Arise, arise, arise!'
'Awaken, awaken, awaken!'
'Wave, wave high the banner!'

the spade into the frozen ground

the black frozen battleground
of the deep shadow of our being, down, towards the root of it now

as the cry
echoes down history
as the cheer goes up for 1900 and 2000

echoes
from John Ball to Brodsky
ANARCHON
raise the black flag! (government is both harmful and unnecessary)
as the voices ring out from the silence

'ye are many, they are few - this is the kingdom of God within man -
 whoever puts his hand on me to govern me is a usurper and a tyrant'

one by one their faces
Shelley, Mary Woolstonecraft and Godwin
Marx, Proudhon and Bakunin
as they parade by in time in seconds

'POWER TO THE IMAGINATION
 LIFE WITHOUT DEAD TIMES, SING THE PROLETARIAT
 man was born free and is everywhere in chains

 flowers for the rebels who failed

 let us put our trust in the eternal spirit'

the cry, the cry, the rallying cry
as we swarm like ants in the face of God
shouts as the ground gives, the flood, of water and blood

the crowded whirlpool rises and froths and sinks again
and again rises time after time and won't be put down -
were we born for this?

sole struggle
mining at the coalface

the dream
awakening to reality
the tragedy

each face I see moulded into form and then broken
the flung fragments of Ixion scattered like chicken flesh
the vulture hovering above Prometheus in chains

the faces blindfolded against the wall - 'Murderers!'

and where did it begin?
how deep the fall that we are so far from our humanness?
from Louis the First to Louis the Five Hundredth
(call a tyrant by any other name he still smells as deathly)

the vast threaded black complexity
the world stage covered in fighting skeletons
their bones crushed to dust under a tunnelling hollow sun

where can it begin?
the ressurrection
the cleansing so great it breaks the bounds of any one of us
(sliding into our birth and death even as I speak)

and the agony of its slowness at the heart of the process
the lingering crucifixion
the timeless moment of the dream ('in the peasant's bent shoulders')

ascent from hell through hell to be healed
and in the knowledge there is no Final Solution
and that 'you can't shoot a fascist with his trousers down'

it begins in anger and is still beginning
I am angry only that the heart is so abused
I refuse to be a statistical non-entity
I refuse to be silenced as I sing and the faggots smoulder under me

the key is power (and the tragedy is power)
of the One over the many until that One rise up within all of us
we are as flies to the gods
we are chained in our unbelief
we are the shadow of our own limitless dying
oppressor and oppressed, we are all
conspirators and victims

from Blackheath to Buchenwald, Armageddon to Aldermaston
the cry echoes under the immemorial blue dome of the sky

waiting for our awakening?
in the one certainty that We Have Made The World And We Must Suffer
It

that much is bloody obvious
although from the sheer weight of unadulterated apathy round here you
wouldn't have guessed it in a millenium

I say it begins right here
in this glimmer of light
animal spirit stirring slowly inside us,
as we touch, without pressure
to possess or fuck, we
touch in the wordless dark, we
sleep together like brother and sister, we
wake with the glimpse of a love
that surpasses the inferno of ego in its simplicity

we resurrect this thing called poetry
in the eye of the hard prosaic city all around us
we hold this living memory

and the ground gives, the spade turns
the gardener kneels on his sack
before the fertile earth
every moment is seeded
fleurs du mal or fleurs du lumière (the choice is ours)

or is it?
I must believe though I cannot name what I believe
I know it is what invisibly fires me
and if I am only another idealist who will dream his dream and disappear

THEN I SHALL DREAM MY DREAM
I will not and cannot just sit here comatose
while the world wheels past me towards catastrophe

I sign on as a member of this Critical Generation
(full time unwaged employment to you, sir)
as England bares its buttocks to America
in the rut root rot of neo-capitalist colonialism
with its robotic claws vamping the Third World dry
for the sake of a meaningless economy

from Washington to Wall Street
don't give a damn, just look after no. 1
fill they belly and bugger thy neighbour

what we cannot deny (if we have eyes to see)
KoreaNamCambodia El Salvador The Lebanon
Afghanistan, Poland, Belfast-Brixton
as a policeman on horseback clips by

and past the primary school squat up the road
its barelit patch-pane mansion front rising
above the freshly sprayed 'eek a mouse' graffitti

WE DEMAND A CONTINUATION OF HISTORY
EALING, DEPTFORD AND HAMPSTEAD CND
EXTINCTION LASTS A LONG TIME

NUKES PUKES
NO CRUI$E (but thanks so much for the offer)

the parade winding
slowly towards Hyde Park

drum-tapping whistle-blowing saxaphone-wailing
as I walk behind a lovely butterfly-stitched banner
with its ode to Mother Courage and People Courage

the raucous raw joy filling the air
jumping up like a jack-in-the-box

'Maggie Maggie Maggie
 out out out!'

To be a revolutionary means you have chosen life

past Downing Street and Cleopatra's monument
the stone finger on top poised like a stationary missile
the entrance to the street barricaded -
to our raised voices and flung insults -

WORKERS POWER THE ONLY WAY
IF YOU WANT PEACE FIGHT AGAINST WAR
as the cartoon hammer of the Kremlin swings down

on a crowd of 'peaceniks' crammed in a (Siberian) tent

DEAR COMRADES, I BEG YOU TO OPEN YOUR EYES
'In Russia, a strike organizer who simply gets fired instead of being
thrown into jail or a work camp is very, very lucky'

REMEMBER THE HUNGER STRIKERS
KILL THE POLICE BILL
'It would be nicer to have a quiet life. But they are not going to let us
have that. If we wish to survive, we must protest'

arise, arise, arise
awaken awaken awaken

THE NUCLEAR STATE IS A TOTALITARIAN STATE
(THERE ARE 135 U.S. BASES ON OUR ISLAND)
'The constant preparations for war further keep violent passions alive
so when a real conflict begins they burst out with renewed vigour. It
thus became possible for an ailing Western power to wage war
enthusiastically with a Third World country over a colonial outpost on
a windswept island. A surge of jingoistic fervour and contempt for
foreigners was easily whipped up by a bloodthirsty press. Some even
insisted: Nuke Buenos Aires!'

NEITHER WASHINGTON NOR MOSCOW BUT INTERNATIONAL
SOCIALISM
BLACK AND WHITE UNITE AND FIGHT
BE REALISTIC! THE RULE OF PROFIT
THE PUBLIC SECTOR IS NOT OURS

DISARM THE RULING CLASS
IF YOU REALLY KNEW
HOW THE ARTS COUNCIL KEEPS IT IN THE FAMILY
WHY I'M VOTING LABOUR

immigration
ratecapping
violence against women

child abuse
Harrington
Nelson Mandela

the list endless from week to week
grand exposé the silver screen flickering
(from VE Day to *Veronika Voss*)

the scouring grey medicine of disillusion
behind the editor's bloodshot aquarium tinted eyes

as I answer back his and my own savage despair with
what are we demanding of ourselves, what
are we acting out of?

I see
disillusion
projection
hatred
virulence
self-righteousness
resentment
self-defence
revenge

I see The Shadow (at the root, in all of us)

the party line's vista of pragmatic emptiness
from Zhdanov to Zero - I say it begins here
(said Danton to Robespierre, in his
 starched stiff white shirt)

I see the trap of reaction we have laid for ourselves
in his leatherclad dialectical skin
swilling his can of toughhead's beer
'Fucking shit beautiful poetry stinks'
rasping out his fucking awful own

I hate Tories
I hate Mars Bars
I hate the middle class

I hate marriage
I hate daffodils
And Mrs Whitehouse is a fart

p.s. I'm wonderful (clap)

and its complex:
'Am *I* your oppressor?', he asked her
to which the reply came, of course you are, white man
despite the fact I've never set eyes on you
I don't even know your name

The only sympathy I can give you is clarity

you are white and middle-class and therefore to blame
(what did you say your name was?)

ογτιε
beyond class and conditioning
a product of both class and conditioning
in chains we label each other with
in minorities we are failing to transcend

I see
the truth we use in cold blood
mirrors the closed nothingness of our hearts
I see
I wouldn't want to live in your brave new world anyway
(and by the way, what world? what vision?)

and its complex:

'The stuff you're writing is bullshit because politics is bullshit. It's all
  unreal. The only thing that's real is inside you'

'Contempt for politics is of course a characteristic Conservative stance'

but what Rosa knew
as she pressed leaves in her prison cell
as she gazed into the eyes of a whipped buffalo
as her murdered body hit the black river water

we need the Tiger
to rout the rottenness
but if the tiger only runs on outrage
what else but this yammering brickbat syntax
liberating us from what?
and into?
and from?

a still muddied source unless we turn within
a source that can only grind on in its groove
of tuneless hopelessness

God save us (from our nihilistic selves)
and yes, Albert Camus
'they blamed on God what they should have blamed on themselves'

I say it begins here
in the heart - and in the shadow of the heart
the rot we secretly feed off,
the shadow we stuff in our closets
bath and mascara and clothe and go out in

We were made better than we make ourselves

and now the healing of the personal
must begin with this
re-valued and re-honoured being
it is ours to live in

lovers, turn inside out -
rebel with a brain -
beyond death and irony -

but first and only through realizing that we are what we see
(and that it is just as counter-revolutionary, comrade, to deny what is
  also inside you)

the key, the crux is
that nothing can change without what is within us
which sustains the very world we cannot change until we begin

at this ending (seemingly, of everything)

'Ideology is one thing. Understanding, unfortunately, is another'

I see
everything around us is dying, our death is a prelude
to the echo of a two thousand year old birth

in this One Long Day that is all one face

the ghost
the voice
that haunts
these extracts:

I am the Free One
struggling to be born in you
I have come through face after face and you have exiled me

as the soul's serene sensing
begins to stir to see slowly through it all
(and at the darkest and deepest,
 the shit that also fosters the seed)
and it's complex

fragile
the upward curve he climbs towards, his wrists gripping and shaking

'There's a natural mystic
 Flowing through the air,
 If you listan care-fully, now
 You may hear'

Politics without spirit is a tunnel without end

There's a natural justice here and now
(in the Way It Happens through what we are)

'The only possibility of coming into real revolutionary power is as
 individuals, as carriers of self-determination and creativity'

and can you say I believe in being human?

as the late bus heaved up Camden Rd.
our faces mute in the dim glow
till the conductor smiled and said something
I forget exactly what it was but it sparked
sudden warmth passing between us, strangers
come in out of the desolate waiting air
and as the bus jolted forward into gear
our elbows touched as we held on
as if we'd known each other all along

I see
how disempowered we are *by ourselves*
I see
how far we are from what is right here in front of us
I see
the illusion of seperation we cling onto & how it kills us
I see
The Lovers standing with The World between them
I see
how we must come back to beauty
I see
that I can choose what I give power to see

the green uprising
outlasting and outliving us
heart-green, and that day at the fair
stalls, kids, and an amateur rockabilly band
mirrored in the glaze of a turquoise vase
and a huge earth mother beaming benificence
with an assortment of pans and spoons tied round her waist

when the heart opens as far as the eyes can see
(you can call it what you like, I call it Being Alive)

I AM PROTECTING LIFE, she said
her just-having-given-birth face
leaning back on the pillow, bathed in stillness
and in these hands as they smooth down
massaging your back and thighs,
and in your body you hesitate to dress
credo quia impossibile est

right here
(speedwell, campion, monk's hood and fuchsia)
in the hovering green
clearing and deepening as the buzzing settles
'Think of the colour, and when you see it, go into it'

feel the plane between your lips
between your body and the ground
between your upper and lower eyelid
lying on a beach in the sun...
feel the sand under your body

feel the light suffuse your skin
see your face now in a mirror
see your body in the sunrise

on this re-awakening planet

'It is faith which matters. Never authority'

as the links of the chain begin to snap

St. Francis, Joseph II, and Gandhi
(beyond est, Exegesis, Rajneesh et al)
and in the park where the march ended
and Frankie Armstrong sang 'We Shall Overcome'
and Kinnock's speech shrank beside her

THIS IS THE REVOLUTION OF ONE AND ONE AND ONE

beyond the holocaust of memory
beyond the riddled complexity
(beyond the myth that only
 our doom-laden desire can save us)

72,000 people at Wembley
as the helicopter camera whirred above the crowd
and he stood there with his fist raised
beside the dazed starving brown-eyed child on the screen
he stood there with his heart open
as it rippled back through us like wind through wheat
the roar quivering up around your head
the sudden indrawn breath from your stomach
catching at the tears moistening the corners of your eyes
(belying the cynical 'now it's cool to be kind')

REMEMBER WHO YOU REALLY ARE
IN THE FREE MIND WE ARE ALL CONNECTED
NEITHER LEFT NOR RIGHT BUT UPLIFTED FORWARD
(NEITHER KINNOCK NOR THATCHER NOR THE SDP)

when we free ourselves
into the greatest fear of all, which is who am I? who are we?
to take on all this in ourselves
to say I am world, one by one
I am the evidence

the self uninjured by time
I am the self that is yours to find
voiced in each second
in each tiny grain of incarnate light
waiting to be released

I am your guide
I am your God
I am your name

and then the darkness fell

what the voices said

and as he fell (back to the train's rocking),
fell back the length of him exhausted on the bed
fell, and floated: fell and dreamt the train
the dim probing lights and curving rails
turning inwards & round

a hand poised holding the thin steel arm
above the swirling grooves
bent forwards, in headphones...
as the stylus touches down

VOICES, FILLING THE DARKNESS
his shadowed head listening

'Angel, are you listening?'
'Just tell me where all this began'
'Not her, not her, not her - but a voice'
'I dreamt I made love with a faceless girl'
'I'm in the dark, but it's OK for the time being'
'I am the strangest child of all'
'I can hear my name being called out far away'
'Which way to the ghost train?'
'All sense of the soul's life rapture, a passionate peace in its blindness
blest'
'The dark I cannot name, the dark I must not name'
'Splinters in the mind of a violent universe'
'They are as curling leaves, and a drying wind blows through them'
'I keep company with the lonely dead'
'I have come to live in a city by the sea'
'Only the dolphins can save me'
'I asked for the rain, and so it does. I am homesick but for another home'
'How I have gone astray!'
'I am afraid this is an awfully muddled letter'
'So continual, this feeling of sliding back and so little forwards'
'I feel in need of long talks'
'The edge of evolution is necessarily in chaos'
'The problem is that we are asleep'
'I suppose I'm not much good at cheering people up. Sometimes I feel
like running away or something'
'I discovered all about black holes on Saturday, they're fascinating. Can
you imagine the infinite gravity pull of the sun if it died?'
'If I could find one place on earth where I could be alone, I think a little
more light might creep into my life'
'Often I feel really Victorian, like when Caryl and I are at home,
articulated, talented Miss So & So's, girls that wrote nature diaries and
were never heard of and died. So I wouldn't mind being there'
'The curtains are open, but I have drawn my face over my face'
'For the first time in my life I'm not sure of what I want'
'I wish there was some way I could stop just existing'
'He is old before his time, and he knows too much'
'Deep down in all of us we long to sleep with all of us'
'Mostly because I am sure I *could* love you very much - if, if, well I don't
know - but not now. And maybe not ever and maybe it would be too
late if I did'
'Of course I haven't forgotten you, I don't forget. Does anyone?'

'Oh my love, thy hair is one kingdom'
'Please therefore do not let your inner quest disassociate you entirely from the externals, or allow the unexplored tunnel to turn into a refuge'...'You got a light, mate?'...'I'm a long way from home, that's all I know'...'And now I can't see where to go, what to do, how even to live'...'She didn't like the mirror, my wife. She said it blocked the light from the window. But you don't look out of the bedroom window much, do you. Draw the curtains and go to bed. Then you get up again. Watch telly and get half pissed. That's your life'...'Can you imagine an exhausted depression crawling over muddy, meaningless days? I never realized I had been so lucky in the past'...'I can hardly understand why I have to go on living; I mean, what does living mean?'...'Christmas is very nice. We all go away for a week and do nothing much, then we all come back and do the same again!'... 'I'm paralysed with boredom'...'I'm a slave in invisible chains'...'Christ, you bastard - he said, yelling at the telephone - I want to break you!'...'Go and find someone new!'...'You say that once more, I said *once more*, do you hear?'...'Fuck off!, eat shit!...'The future: spit!'...'This is a fuck of a pen'...'Well, you see, Jonathan decided he was going to punch him. And that was the end of the problem'...'We are in the asshole of the '80's. Money is spent for raising warships from the bottom of the sea (bugger the Mary Rose, they want to raise the Antelope and the Atlantic Carrier next). Victory parades in front of the Stock Exchange, Bank, Mansion House that resemble Red Square - missiles, tanks and armoured cars in *our* streets, today, this very day, at precisely one o'clock'...'Not even banking could surpass the incessant fiscal concerns of this company. Each single action, word is calculated financially. Each second has a cost, each person, each thing'...'Sod the flowers, sod the trees, it's people, isn't it?'...'I've just seen my first scarecrow for years. He stood, sullen and grubby - crucified so that man can extract every last ounce from the earth'...'I spit on life that does not listen to life'...'I'm an idiot, am I? No, only intellectuals are idiots'...'I can say what I want and no one will hear me'...'Death is taboo, love is taboo, pain is taboo - but anger is anger'...'They don't understand that this country isn't something abstract; it's us; each bloody person crawling on this bloody spot of earth'...'Think of the number of forests that have gone into what has been written'...'The last time I saw Mark he was sitting outside calmy in a beaten up armchair smoking a joint and watching a pile of televisions he had just set fire to'...'It was a craze in the 1940's, it spread like wildfire. They called it 'balloon hopping'. People were jumping over buildings!'...'If you think I'm radical, wait until you meet my brother Paul'...'I tell you it's all rubbish and it's got to go'...'Please forget I was ever called David Rowan'...'I can't say how I am since that implies logical sentences and I'm incapable of them'...'To live it requires being mastered by the

force of life itself'...'I'm a pretty useless person, but in Him I have all the resources I need'...'She even takes her knickers to the rabbi'...'Can't a man accept freely, these days?'...'Why don't you feel me up while I'm reading my book'...'What do my glasses make me look like? I think they make me look like a metallurgy teacher'...'As the test pilot said, I'm lost but I'm making record time'...'Is it far to Nakhabia?'...I can't help what I say...not in my voice sings the fish in the net...I am the dead body under the floor, I talk...there are three people in my head when I talk...abstract language saves them from desire...oh swan, you are rare and endangered...She refuses to be isolated and remains unfathomable, my sentences crash in the darkness and lie scattered on the paper...I feel this body like a prison. I feel everything like that but my mind...So I crack jokes and act whatever the part is that's acceptable, because myself isn't...I live on only for the sake of the unrealized spirit...I slip too easily into eternity and always have to pay for it...My bright body is bleeding inside my head...I drew a note in gold and it broke...I need to be enveloped and envelop...I would add, I have no other life but this...I don't trust my words, I don't know who you are, taking them in, I don't know who I am, who this mouthpiece is; at the moment; talking's betrayed me, it's dark night...it sounds Arabic to me, I think we've got a crossed line...is there any way out of here?... There is no face which can answer your questions...If I let go, the world won't hold me...I can't see the map, its too dark...am I murdering the world, or is it murdering me?...I had visions and they killed me... he was out of breath, his lungs were aching, he had no choice, he had to swim or he'd drown, into the blackness ahead, through the pitch black water, with the rock walls either side of him, and the tangling weeds under him...swim or he'd drown...mouth clenched...blood behind his goggles... aaaaah! aaaaaaaaaah! aaaaaaaaaaah!...till the darkness cracked and he came through in an explosion of green light

!

'God, the most blinding self awareness'
'AAAAAAH! AAAAAAAH! AAAAAAAAAAAH!'
'He was always impatient to live in spirit'
(*the screams continue*)

'With ideals like that you're bound to suffer'
'I know now why Nietsche went mad. Simple fact - he couldn't pray'
(*the screams continue*)

'Perhaps my falling in love with you was a vigil, and when you realize

111

it's hopeless, your pain will cease'
(*the screams continue*)

'I feel that its taken us all this time to come to know each other, and now
it's all for nothing'
'I feel nothing for you but flat shadow. Goodbye'
(*they begin to subside*)

'Yes it does end. However long the ending is'
'I want to get back...I want no more missing years'
'The brink is still too damn near'
(*the voices begin to fade. Pause. The dim crackling of static. Then slowly
out of the silence, the sound of waves breaking on a shore*)

'How hard should I try? to let be'
'I see I've been clouting myself with stormclouds'
'Did I say that? Did I really say that?'
'Touch me where it hurts and grows'
'I couldn't read. I kept hearing the sound of a violin in the rain'
'I am holding onto something I am begging to be released from'
'Take the one journey to the heart, my friend'
'I want magic and I am afraid of it'
'As the sun sets and where the day ends each day is what is right'

(*the waves begin to recede, to the sound of wind through leaves*)

'I am a woman coming up out of very deep water'
'I am a gold medallion coming up out of the darkness'
'I am a candleflame, a crystal, a strong white light'
'I never knew my soul could feel so beautiful'
'Stronger now? Yes. Also humbler'
'I need the world and the world needs me'
'I need to dance to express my love'
'And I undid the chains around me'

(*the sound of the leaves stills, and through the wind comes the voice of
a woman singing wordlessly in an unknown language. Behind her voice,
the wind and the waves begin to echo softly*)

'From the other side: that is what wishes to be heard now: that the gates
of death are down'

...as the room filled

its air vibrating soundlessly
the glimpsed white figure
standing over him
his hand resting
for a moment on his shoulder
touching the crown
of his slumped head
as the record circled round

         and round...

> **livid darkness**

Black flame -

and the dim sound
of dipping oars,
black flame!

       curling round

            a falling body

'It was during Advent of the year 1913 - 12th December, to be exact - that
I resolved upon the decisive step. I was sitting at my desk once more,
thinking over my fears. Then I let myself drop...'

a plummetting cross

the torn gold chain
her throat bared
her eyes squeezed shut

- the train crashing its brakes too late
her falling
                    fainting
                              crushed steel scream

ripping across the torn air
flung hair, pushed from inside from behind

and the sprig of lavender
twisted in still warm
silver paper
he kneels to pick up

It all happened so suddenly -
I had no idea -
There was nothing we could do, she just -

**THE NORTHERN LINE SERVICE HAS BEEN SUSPENDED DUE TO
A PERSON**

oh my God

'all words and phrases are too mild'

I must go ahead now, having no wit to protect me and no knowledge.
Into the dark where only my eyes can peer and my ears listen. Down
and down, clutching my voice to me, retaining nothing but the few skills
I've acquired on my previous journeys. But this time I must go the whole
way, go deeper than breath, believing only that this is my last chance,
with the air all around pressing down on my strength. The opening can-
not be far away now

the sign points
to the centre of this dark core

I feel so heavy I could fall through the ground

I am naked, running across a dark land
drops of black rain staining my skin

falls
        through his mind

's eye expanding
                like a giant full stop

too late to turn back   as the coach drifts
the motorway stretching northwards   into the blackness
rain streaking the windscreen   hunched over the wheel
'Was that the way out there?'
'We've missed the turning'

it begins in normality
just under the stretched skein of the surface
the wet slippery tarmac
where the fuse
                smoulders
deep
        into the dark

the path narrowing into shadow
...figures emerging,
all very young:
the girls with heavy make-up
and the boys leaning
pushing out their legs
their crotches stuffed with padding
(as one of them leaves
 with a man in a cabaret raincoat)

black flame
                ghost-real
                        livid dark

reeling   frame by frame

as I sat by the window
and a woman's cry
from Lakeside Rd.
pierced my reflection

'Thus he speaks with tears, and gives his ship full sail'

sitting alone in a dark empty cinema
my eyes as if in 3D fusing with the shifting screen
(They fuck. The television is on in the background)

Lenny Montana is executed in *The Godfather*
Richard Widmark is fatally wounded in *Madigan*
John Vernon is flung from penthouse apartment terrace
by Lee Marvin in *Point Blank*

inching - slowly - along the ledge - of a high building
the city lights - plunging - sixteen storeys
                                        below

In New York City When The Lights Went Out
- panic sounds
- people stuck in lifts
- rooms with windows that wouldn't open

and into the black silence where no planes could land

'If you want to know how much darkness there is around you, you must
  sharpen your eyes, peering at the faint lights in the distance'

(the tense lunar air -
  sirens going everywhere -
  your fixed white face
  in line at the petrol station)

at Camden Town
waiting for the last train south,
the soot stained walls in the dim light
as he paced up and down the platform's length
ruffled greasy hair and pinched face
broken shoes and lurid orange anorak
his arms swinging wildly at his sides...
silent, pretending to read his book
the print blurring deeper with each shout
silent, with still nine minutes before the train

and the trail of strangled dogs he left behind him

'But Daedalus, pitying the violent love of queen Ariadne, unravels to
  Theseus the intricacies and windings of the structure, himself guiding
  his dark mazy steps by a thread'

a hair's breadth
less & less -

unless we, if we, when we
if we ever

'Get out! I want this station to myself! you bloodsuckers! Can't you leave
  me in peace!'

the scream
welling inside him
the cry so deep
only the sky's whole invisible dark face could hear it

beside the alien's message home ringing in his brain
INSANITARY HUMANITY PROFANITY CALAMITY

stripped layer by layer
character by character
till I am not even oγτιε I am just plain no one
'You got two bob, son?'

the nightmare of the thing
                                    infinitely repeated
fall after fall after fall
                        90,900,9000

that the mind cannot contain
spread all around him, covering the floor
piled in boxes and marked with innumerable slips of paper

'Are you the Director?'
'Yes I am. Sit down'
(they exchange glances)
'Now, have you brought the script with you?'

dreams the one book he needs
Dismantling The Shadow
brand new,
                wrapped in light cellophane

slipping past his outstretched hands and out of reach -

falling after it
as the old wino

     shrugs and walks away

his question unanswered

the ground beneath his feet beginning to quiver
rippling downwards

       through the valley his figure

silhouetted, as he begins to walk

as if casually to the end of the platform

and then down

    between the rails

         and in

his full bags weighed either side of him:

'Wait a minute. This might be the beginning, I'm not sure'
(*begins leafing through the unnumbered pages*)

and the voice whispering

     begin to let go

the key falling past him,
his outstretched figure

the typewriter falling out of the window
as the camera pans down into the street he is walking
the wet glow of the pavement behind his steps
the streetlight's blur like a white planet

LONDON DUSK TO DAWN

wandering

Black flame. Dark windows parked cars empty streets

'The city favours brief and furious outbursts, but not the long haul.
Moreover for all its drama and existential fury, or perhaps because of
it, it's a city where it can remarkably hard - or so it seems to me - to
get on the right side of one's despair'

close up to moving
head in shadow and shoulders:
blur to darkness...

...each image come through
the back of his head
and out from in between his eyes

'*To the centre of the city where the roads meet...*'
Suicide Bridge,
rising above the road
the falling figure
            suspended in mid air

noosed,
hanging in a room
the piled manuscript
            beneath his swaying straw body

burning stench
of bitumen and sulphur
burning sound
          in the rocking carriage

lurching as the lights dim on and off
her pink wig and sugar-white face
white ruff and rouged lips
queen's thin fingers
           covered in rings

the fantasy for real
gazing awkwardly askance
dream-doll, astral dream image
             hovering on the empty seat

'O Thou vampire Queen of the Flesh, wound as a snake around the throats
of men! I adore Thee, Evoe! I adore thee, IAO!'

'O Thou fierce whirlpool of passion, that art sucked up by the mouth
of the sun! I adore thee, Evoe! I adore thee, IAO!'

walking on the Heath
to the edge of one of the paths there

where she points in silence
to the daubed symbol of a crucified toad
grinning in the tingling black stillness

- evil

his priapic prick lunging forward
his spittle voice
                    incanting and snapping

'Stab your demoniac smile to my brain
 Soak me in cognac, cunt, and cocaine'

- evil

touched, tugged on his arm
by the split-second cloaked figure
pouring white paint over the black cock's screech
as the cornered Ripper crashes backwards through the glass

'Yes gods, to whom the empire of ghosts belong'
do you know what you're asking for?
'and ye silent shades, and Chaos, and Phlegethon'
if you get stuck here, you're done for
'permit me to utter the secrets I have heard'

'Hence is a path, which leads to the floods of Tartarean Acheron'

the hollow sound of his echoing laughter
clamours around his cupped ears
turning the walkman up

'But this is madness'
'Well, you said you wanted to film the inside of his mind'
'But it's technically impossible!'
'I can assure you, Mr. Big, it's 100% real'
(*the Director lights a Marlboro and ponders*)

turning over in his mind
the violent mist thrown up by two bodies -
a child screaming in Waitrose *waa-a-ah*!
the thick green light in a Dungeons & Dragons hologram

O Father Gaufridi!
as she falls to the floor
writhing and dancing
Suck me!
   Sabbats!
      Sodom!
neighing like a horse

the flame burning behind his eyes
walking forward with his aura blazing
as the face of Gale Parsons looms
with its dry lips and junkie-brown eyes
crouched in a kitchen, her clenched bare knees
her hair covering her face tilted over the syringe

'Where do you think you're heading, Gale?'
'To die, I suppose'
'To die?'
'Yes'
'But you're only nineteen. You have an IQ, they say, of 120'
'Mmm, that's what they say'
'And you're pretty'
'Awful'

stretched out his hand
to touch her tear-streaked
charcoal-black - shouting, *No!*
leaving an X marked on the palm of his hand

THIS IS THE REALM OF AHRIMAN

in the 4 a.m.
cold blue gaslit hour
     her black words scratch through

twenty years later, still being written
the undead undried ink

'Dark tunnel through which hurtle the visitations
 The visitations, the manifestations, the startled faces.
 I am the centre of an atrocity'

I am

the blind man
victorian
bohemian
narrator
the lover
the rebel
the joker

'I am Peace, I am Jesus, I am Tutankhamun!'
hung on the Easter crucifix up on Parliament Hill
roped hands and feet above the neon flicker

as the sky explodes in technicolor

the crowd waits
as the bare chested actor
flicks the bottle down on the cobblestones
holding the smashed neck
as he invites the audience
to come and trample all over him

the cracked whip singeing the air
as he holds the newspaper open in front of him
and she shreds it inch by inch without touching him
turning her black leather hips and slow defiant smile

the edge that cuts these shadows
clicking from his wrist, the blade dancing
open in a flash of strength
above the hauling sinking heart
the trawling dragged corpse of all these deaths

into the depth-dark
shark silent light, tightrope balanced
razor's edge height

sucking under him
                    smouldering under him

in the red shadows a hundred feet
beneath street level,
the hunched figures around the fire
holding four skewered monster rats

the child's horrified fascinated voice
'I saw the female eating the male, mummy
 I saw the brain!'

I hear Lord B., despite his crippled condition
still managed to drive out every day in the Rover
and blast out of the window at any living thing he saw

I pass his rotting blooded face being eaten by foxes
I pass the face of a broken Samaritan
still holding his 'phone receiver
as he beckons to tell me
how the father buggers the son
how the boy finds the father in bed with his 13yr. old sister

I pass the poet
staring into the soul of Faustus
I pass the actor
with his face against a bleached white tree
I pass the soon-to-be-dead Director
in his felt hat slumped across the wheezing black sofa

as he walks
              struck dumb beside me...

eyes front, just keep walking straight ahead
as the zombie on the other side of the street
lingers in his metallic suit and dark glasses
with an armful of beer bottles he stops
one by one
              to hurl against the hoardings

pacing in his pork pie hat and track shoes
a petrol bomb poised in his right hand
frozen as he swings it from his eyes and clenched mouth
'Hey man, what you see...no, you too late for the REAL burning'
as the soundtrack begins

'I don't know who did me, or why'
'He hit me twice. There was blood on my hair'
'He kicked the door in and started bashing me'
'The kids who did this are the kind I try to help'
'They got Chris across the throat with a brick and slashed his neck'

as Leatherface grabs his victim from behind
and the dim voice of sanity observes

screeching tyres - police sirens - horns
running feet - voices rasping and shouting

rushing rails - fists - and gun shots
uh! ah! uh! ah!

'You're right. We're two of a kind'
'Oh Ja-mes'

eyes glued to the video
the screen reflecting the seated passengers

I wake from this dream of hell only when the screen is blank

as all along the carriage the silence breaks
the standing crushed bodies break out

'Fuck!'
'You smell of shit!'
'Spunk in your hair!'
'You soulless trendy!'
'Louse-arsed punk!'
'Fascist pisshead!'
'Seal-skin cow!'
'Bow-legged dog!'
'Yuppie muppet!'
'Come here and say that!'
'Worm eater!'
'Brownhatter!'
'Vim sniffer'
'Moron!'

There was an old pimp called Rodney
Who provided the best prod in Putney
Till Rod went beserk
And purchased a skirt
Now his arsehole is running with chutney!

heavy sighs - rushing flame - breaking glass
drunken shouts - farts - a pulled lavatory chain

'Here we go, here we go, here we go-o'

'I like to see a man really suffer'
'Hang him! that's what they should do'
'The insult that made a MAN out of me'
'Pervert! Paedophile! Plebiscite! Ppp!'
'Coming, sir? thick or thin, sir?'
'Nigger. White Trash. Nigger. White Trash'
'Do you want power?'
'You pathetic cringing little toad!'

as a girl bangs on the carriage door
'The door's not opening, the door's not opening'

and nobody moves

as the sound cuts

and on screen

a huge black fingerprint emerges

KILLERS LEFT DEATH TRAIL ACROSS AMERICA

Kenneth Bianchi and 'Steve Walker'
Alton Coleman and Debra Brown

Hindley, Brady, Sutcliffe, Nilsen

as he kneels by the path
$\qquad\qquad$ and retches, vomits

the moorland's death surrounding him
at the mist-laden end of the lightless road

the backward glance of the handcuffed killer
NO. 13 DIED IN THE BATH
looking like a faculty librarian
the chilling 160 page statement
I scanned and scanned his face for
traced along the line of his sealed mouth

the boiled heads

the 'games with corpses'
the blocked drains
the hysterical jokes
the, the

unnameable unutterable whisper that fills him

as he sees the figure on the screen
in a long grey coat, black hat and bricklayer's boots

        slowly coming into focus
        becoming slowly familiar,
     although the face remains dark
       as it walks towards him
   he finds himself walking towards it
    he finds himself walking in it

staring up at a high lit window
the shadow crosses and recrosses, naked
the bag of chips cooling in his hand
his shadow falling in front of him as he walks
step for step haunting the street

'I'm afraid there isn't anyone here called David'
'Never mind. You sound like a nice man'
'Are you sure you've got the right number?'
'Sure. I'm Marcella. I'm not far away'

'At the third stroke it will be 9.46 and 30 seconds'

'This is the end
Beautiful friend
This is the end
My one and only friend
It hurts to set you free
But you'll never follow me

The end of laughter and soft lights
The end of nights we tried to die

This is the e-n-d'

```
┌─────────────────────────┐
│                         │
│                         │
│         death           │
│                         │
│                         │
└─────────────────────────┘
```

'Be not fond of the dull, smoke-coloured light from Hell. That is the path
which openeth out to receive thee because of the power of accumulated
evil *karma* from violent anger. If thou be attracted by it, thou wilt fall
into the Hell-Worlds; and, falling therein, thou wilt have to endure
unbearable misery, whence there is no certain time of getting out'

- flame die,
the lashing hissing
voices in his mind he walks through

scene after scene in these descending circles
the-one-incident-so-dark-it-could-break
your-faith-forever
(the blinded father crawling
towards the son's loaded shotgun,
the dragnet his hand is slowly releasing)

'Come back!' 'Cop out!' 'Dead head!'

shouts and accusations pursuing him
break around his being and bounce off
bleed around his eyes,
                        scream around his heart
tug at his ankles,
                    and up around his thighs

the blackness blazing inside his mind
burns to the core it strangely cannot penetrate
as long as he keeps walking
some part of him

the unnamed
somehow
godknows sustaining

his death-clouded cells
the power flooding into him
and where the path will fork
at the crossroads beside the gallows tree

that can feel everything and break
and yet not break; be so unnamed
he becomes almost unrecognizable tramp-shadow
and yet, stripped so, the other begins
to reveal the him that is really real

as the flame dies,
creeping along the match's length
consumed in black, curling, bent
its head like a tar brush
flung onto canvas - dipped in river blood
the ghostly imprint under a photocopier
the eyes' closed grainy living death mask

as the whirling newsprint collage ashens
the riot of headlines, soaked in the slush
he wades with his torch through
under the dripping roof

'Lighten our darkness we beseech thee O Lord'

WE ARE THE DEAD
WE HAVE MURDERED THE DEEPEST MYSTERY OF ALL
AND WHAT HEALTH IS THERE IN US?

the final cry
                in the dream
                                as the ground begins to tremble

Aberfan, 1963
as the heap began to move
silently down through the mist

hung for a moment
                in the sunlit blue air

'Children were waving up at the plane'

8.16 on the blasted watch face

- the flung shadows
- the soundtrack gone silent
the excavated frieze

a man found propped up reading a newspaper,
two children at the school entrance, hand in hand
a woman sculpted in the laval dust
above the one surviving child

the village crumbling stone by stone
                                        into the sea

the page held up to the wavering beam:

'A slip had lately taken place when I was there yesterday morning. The
earth was fresh, and black, huge blocks of the old monastery had tumbled
with it and the end of the chancel wall seemed to hang over above, as
though its hour had come. But from the black earth and yellow sand
gaunt bones protruded - not one but dozens. Every time the earth falls
a tomb opens, and it grisly contents are precipitated onto the beach. I
counted a score of fragments of human limbs, there a thigh bone, there
a part of a pelvis, and there, perched on a mound of earth and masonry,
a broken, toothless skull, the sockets where the eyes had been staring
out on the restless waters'

he die
she die
we die

the fallen postbox up the road
lying in a spray of bits of sunlit shattered glass
as the circle turns

around the passing faces, in a snack bar
from mirror walking to mirror - as transient as thought
the way each face fades, from face to face
through his face above the drained coffee cup

'The lonely one who looks on,

The bearer of human longing, the pale image'

The Lightning Struck Tower

and as the huge metal ball

                        swings, against the brickwork

'I must grasp as one invisible reality source and ashes, lips and a
  dead rat'

dead dream
of the Master
in a forest clearing

seven foot grey-boned in an army greatcoat
skull and set teeth as he walked
his steps looming soundless through the bracken

and his dog
lying dead by Camden Lock
the red bus front's blind eyes had struck
in his belly and blood-stained muzzle, gone still
stiller than breath, sky still -
the caught passing throats fighting for air
the rounding steps and averted faces
and everything else blurred but his black fur
and the river of air flowing inside me
and the skeleton of the city everywhere around me

'Mummy is going away on a long journey'
'God loved Johnny so much he wanted him in heaven'

the Mortlake hearse in the rear view mirror,
the road curving round the cemetery

and the stories,
the glossed lips and dusted white skin
- an entire family buried
under glass round a dinner table -
Mr Joyboy at your service, sir
we'll fix her up as good as new (wink wink)
silicone breasts and scented pubis
starting with a smile like *this*, see

(his fingers tugging back his cheeks)
to say nothing of the Frozen Generation awaiting release!
(sorry guys, we've all gone to another planet
ps: fishfingers in the fridge)

Mrs Phoebe Crow
who died May 28 1817 aged 77 years
who, during 40 years
as a midwife in this City
brought into the world
9730 children

.

Robert Lives Esq.
a Barrister
so great a lover of peace
that when a contention arose
between Life & Death
he immediately yielded up
the Ghost
to end the dispute
Aug. 12th 1819

.

Here lies
in a horizontal position
the outside case of
Thomas Hinde
Clock & Watchmaker
who departed this life wound up
in hope of being taken in hand
by his Maker and being
thoroughly cleaned repaired and
set a-going in the world to come

.

Valentine Snow
Thaw every breast
Melt every eye with woe
Here's dissolution

By the hand of Death!
To dirt, and water turned
The fairest snow
O the King's Trumpeter
Has lost his breath

Death, so that the last thing that is certain is no longer?

branches frozen
in the ice of a winter sky

'It feels like there's a maggot in my third eye'

chrysalis
butterfly
its moth wings
opening behind the window
the word dissolves into

struggling back from the dead of sleep
lungs like a fish crawling out of the water

as he walks towards the threshold

horses' hooves
                crushed beetles
                                whale's intestines
boiled pig, a baby's
bawling bald red head by a meat stall

dust to dust
skin for skin
an I for an I

and is that light, shining?
(as she sets the small rosebush
 among the green glazed gravel)
and in the flute-sound she died in?
the blaze of symphonic music he went out in?
the speakers lying
                       either side of his ears
her body
               falling into the High Street shopping crowd

the day's obituary in his glass of whisky
and dark glasses, suddenly old

                      walking along the greensward

and Joe, the castle caretaker
with his sparse white hair and Newcastle accent
'That's you', holding out his palm
'No one else has these lines'
'And well, you may win the pools
 Or be hit by a bus, but you never diverge for long:
 That's your reason...'
'And that's Joe', he said, gesturing to the last page
'This was Joe'

the pathos of her handwriting
wishing she could get to within sight of the sea
'But my hip won't let me'

and 'I have to tell you the sad news that Andy (of Andrew's Cafe)
died a couple of weeks ago. He had a heart attack in the shop front'

and at Dingwalls that time
with the disco over and the bar closing
in his creased blue denim shirt & jeans
wandering forlornly around the dance floor
trying to get close to any woman who could stand him,
stumbling dazed past the edge of a table
crouched by the PA with his head in his hands

and in Paris, the street crowd surrounding him
a wiry, tanned Algerian about to risk his act
requesting francs: stopped, and said very quietly
'Don't throw pebbles, I'm not part of the pavement'

and the father distraught at the press conference
his daughters found raped in a roadside ditch
pleading with the killer to reveal his name
'If I got my hands on him, I'd strangle him'

as she sang

*'I just dropped in
 To sa-y, how much I care'*

slurring her drunken tearful face
as the passengers looked sideways and down
and in the silence between each burst of song
'That's what my life was'

the heart
the death we all carry
the cripple in a wheelchair
                           with his throat working
the postcard
               inked in green:

'Florence is still beautiful
 Even without us.

 I tried, I lost'

the fallen now snow-covered leaves
the frozen winter bird crying heart
seeing through the darkness and into this

the returned parcels
                     simply 'Deceased'
consoling voices
                chatting in clichès

lay under the tree
                  with the leaves drifting
                                  down on him
lay
      past hope of anything
lay
      with his eyes closed in the spectral sun
lay
      the corpse of him become a line
lay
      and began to let everything go
lay
      so light he could have been floating
lay
      as the ground took his pain from under him
lay
      until I stirred inside him

and she said: 'We learn that we have never lived'

and she said: 'I can be hell as long as I know where my love is'

and she said: 'I knocked softly. There was no answer. She'd gone. I left her as she was, lying peacefully with her hands folded and her eyes closed. I find this very hard to describe, but when I returned, the atmosphere of the room had changed. It was charged, charged with grace. I crossed the threshold, and...*she came to meet me*, the room filled and welled with her presence, which was clearer and stronger and more spacious than when I'd known her alive. And her face on the pillow had a look of deep quiet triumph, of completion. It was beautiful'

the unknown

'I know that I hung
 On the windswept tree
 For nine whole nights
 Pierced by the spear
 And given to Odin -
 Myself given to myself
 On that tree
 Whose roots
 No one knows

They gave me not bread

Nor drink from the horn;
Into the depths I peered,
I grasped the runes,
Screaming I grasped them
And then fell back'

...to what begins at the end of everything. The edge. He will walk out
here, he will walk right through the dream with his rucksack and tent,
and make his home here in an outhouse, a shed

- blackness. The ground still beneath him. Twilight. Everyone is going
home. The edge of night. The unknown. The sky. The always anywhere
anytime strangeness closening

tranced and tantalizing. The lines of force binding and weaving the whole
so vast - the stars you always end up losing count of. Do you know what
I mean? do you know who I am? we are?

- his head reflected in the curving dome of a coloured marble: shadowed
lips, and eyes, aquiline nose and forehead rising back, moving back,
slowly floating back, detached, distanced to a dot of blue lamplight

the sky reaching above him, the clouds slowly dissolving, with the flicker-
ing lights below, the moon rising, the evening star - and for a moment
it is the sky he is lying on and the city he is gazing up at

the bridge that only a blind man leading two white donkeys could cross,
and the mosque, from memory, rising in its filigree of a million particled
pieces of square blue mosaic the candlelight began as if to loosen

each stone a face, each stone a star: in my finally empty face, the marble's
clear opaque depth, turning, spiralling, and like a magnet, drawing him
towards its four dimensional mirror

the dreamer, the traveller inside this unknown inner fluid body moving
down its endless tunnel of dreams - seeking...in that goddess-garden
place, where her hair became a part of everything that was growing there
...and above her bright uplifted face, a huge kite-sized black butterfly
rose above the trees, the only one of its kind

- blackness, the mirrored writing dissolves in, the few remaining phrases
snatched from sleep: and the mountain, collapsing in on itself, the
climbing figure pitched into descent

The only thing that ever makes me think is the feeling that I don't understand anything anymore

I am a shadow in a mirror. The rest is all eyesight and insight

I am the telling of an untold story

...as if born here like Romulus, dark child of the universe, the sky's thighs clenching and contracting, opening and withdrawing, leaving him abandoned, *tabula rasa*, groping over his abacus, peering at the world through his tiny intellectual mind!

alone with the stars, the stars filling his brain with their gelatinous haunting light...spiralling throughout the universe

pulsars quasars red giants white dwarfs: the same violence out of which we were made...star-body...star-brain...shining down a five hundred foot tunnel

become a thirty-three inch cool white observatory disc, behind which...the vast mathematics of light years, whole histories of feeling...expanding and co-existing...

and the eclipsed sun's corona like an irradiant dilated eye...that the Milky Way spirals into...a black mirroring marble...a face slowly coming into focus beyond which

the black drop beyond which nothing has begun to exist...and the echo of the beginning wound back on film, infinitely receding...from where the light curves towards us from across the remotest horizon

Andromeda, the Crab, Orion and Centaurus...Cygnus A, 3C273 and M87...to where your eyes meet the hairs on the back of your neck...to where 'beyond which' becomes 'in which'

the sole unnameable essence begins to stir, at the depth of the mind massed in on itself...step by step become heavier and heavier...step by step as its eight-mile disc turns red

becomes black, and steps through itself inwards...towards the edge of a glittering softer than white sea

'I then decided I would try and reach a certain ruined temple in Tibet of which my master, Azelda, had spoken. With this end, I concentrated my will in one big effort, expecting to rush off in some horizontal direction. The result was absolutely unexpected. The ground collapsed beneath my feet and I was falling, with seemingly tremendous velocity, down a dark narrow tunnel or shaft. This downward descent continued until I lost my time sense and it seemed that I might have been falling for hours. Something in me was getting frightened, but I managed to keep calm by telling myself I was really in bed in Wimbledon and that my Master would protect me. At last I came gently to rest. Blackness and silence, then, as one awakening from a heavy sleep, I became progressively aware of my surroundings'

Dark reality where the dreams stop

It is dark. You are wide awake

- on this edge of time and space, spelt letter by letter, the tapping keys, passed by in the lit square of window above, the stars above the roof, the sky turning silently out beyond his glass thin reflection, his skin, covering him, porous, leaking space, the giddiness of it, he stands silhouetted against, like a question mark, etched in smoke... the sense that seeps through his standing, hardly even aware of himself there, gone so deep into listening

from where the light fell back, the sunlit daylit Heath that afternoon, walking out across the grass, the homing wood pigeon's echo still lingering from years before, around his step by step opening, and the houses mirrored in the pond water, the air waiting all around him, where he lies down on the grass, the garden grass become this grass: and the blank open pages of a notebook, and the stub of a pencil moving across the lines, the whispering still voice in his inner ear, behind which...I am him...where we overlap...in that shaded area...where we touch, he writes

*lived life, no kind of theory...the fact is only the lightest can touch...*the phrased breath filling him, and in what he is seeing...*the visible synchronicity of things, gentleness, a mound of green, and dreaming human beings*...a kite flying high in the blue stillness, its thread stretching taut and slack between his eyes...the kite his grounded body...his eye...the sky...where the sky in his mind touches its expanse...*right in front of your eyes is what is hardest and simplest to realize*...the vivid, lit transparent air...the detail of everything sharpening and quickening, second by second unfolding...*in which death and life are one word, one understanding, one and every face*...the curved hill's sky space rising

138

above the vacant bench...two runners cross, leaning over their flexed elbows and legs...*Nature is what moves as we could, should, be moving...* the water, rippling, the leaved trees' light rustling...the slow steps of someone passing him...*first in your body, then out into the body...*lying close to the ground, with his head on one side...*and because your suffering brings you closer, far closer, I applaud it...*two women, nearby him, sleeping side by side...the pencil moving almost imperceptibly...*always negation to reach beyond...*two swans, their wings shaped back, their necks lowered, drifting back and forth...back into the dream-time...*on our way through what our eyes know to be unreal...*the sunlit city almost far away...the grass prickling his face, the ground holding him in its balance...*I can feel your thought inside me, and I am trying to explain it as I speak...*crystal simplicity, syllable by syllable...the windows of the mansion block shimmering in the distance...the vague sound of bells building up to tell the time...*moving lightness, carrying this light inside you; the way you move, the way you do what you mean...*the bells' echo, the pause, in which the hour never struck...the voice held open...curving like the sun...towards the deep return

bestillbesilentbeslowbestrong

in the light he came down from,
cracked white, straining to break through
the force of it one night filling his room
the pain of it in his uneven eyes and face
as he came to the threshold and was flung back -

into the dead hovering dark street
his sheer nakedness tense to every sound
his head pounding with its intensity
on the edge of a universe so vast and vertiginous
a glimpse of worlds opening laying within layer
at the tip of which, the bare beginning of which
is the place we live here...behind which

Angel, Self, daemon, guide
the thin incarnate dotted eggshell of being
linked from its star-sketched third eye crown
to where the contents of our mind are created, living,
real - no longer myths, but entities
breathing their life through from behind our eyes
behind which...

(as a smoke-like substance spirals up from the body of a dying bird)

edim   daena   atman   ruah

psyche - nous - thymos

anima divina

the do re me fa so of this octave
a lost universal language of light
a voice chanting om mani padme hum

sense of presence
unity (oneness)
sense of guidance
response to prayer
by way of music or art
inarticulate
implosion
out of the body
e.s.p.
unclassified

Socrates, standing in silent day and night meditation
Shackleton tracking the ice with his invisible fourth companion
Ted Serios staring the image of a building into a camera

behind which...the minutiae of charged electron particles, enclosed in
a space-time of increasing negentropy, spreading from within the human
form and its encoded past present and future totality -

summa behind which...something moves him towards letting it all go,
the wa hè gu ru, the great fugal pattern...the rose light sunset sky and
the lower pond's reflection of a sign blanked out white, no word visible,
no word audible, as the space begins to open

begin fingering this piano, the way he listens over it with his head bent,
his white hair and sightless eyes

- the prelude is almost finished. It will soon be time to go. You are here
for what you don't know

and the thing, with half the keys missing, and the pedals broken off,
every note echoic

and nearby, the upus tree which poisons everything in its shadow

'But one forgets. And if there is only one he will depart all alone, towards
his master, and his long shadow will follow him, across the desert, it's
a desert, that's news, Worm will see the light in a desert, the light of
day, the desert day'

as the train emerges marked SPECIAL, its obscured black windows, its
slow creaking on the empty platform as its middle carriage doors open
to admit one passenger

where has he come from?

that lonely young man walking the night streets,
his wraith on the adjacent platform at South Ken
he stared back in weary amazement at -
pale and unfed, unloved and unliving
and three years later

his hidden self in the Hotel Henri IV
Dionysiac the morning after, sitting by the balcony
his face leaning back into the unexposed darkness
his arm and hand casually balanced on the railing
the square of daylight on the church through the shutters
- you know all this

Jekyll and Hyde face: one part light and smiling
the other either stoned, or as cold as stone
the line running down his forehead and nose
behind which...
ah yes

mechanical lust animal dogging his eyes,
the priest with his white intellectual skin
the madman crouched by a bare white wall
the aesthete with his charming manipulative grin
as they fuse together from where he has trodden
his steps invisibly haunting him

in the shadow he begged to be released from, would deny, would turn
on, would shout out loud inside *why? I don't want to be this, I don't
want to live this, it isn't what I came here for, it isn't what I came here
to be*

and still it persisted...page after page...tunnelling deeper and deeper...
into the world of rank matter...the yoke of mortal living...dead filth and
horror and unredeemed misery - dragging its gravity through him (little
David with a pebble in his sling and a blindfold round his eyes)

and through every step I guided him, skin after skin in his gradual self-
encompassing, and in each moment where he knows nothing, and is most
here, most open, most heart:

To be standing still
Here on this earth
With a vision
You thought you had completed

To be standing still
Here on this earth
With the whole of it
Unfinished

and now I stand aside...

Long ending alone. I don't know. The snow falling, flaking down.
Strange over everything. Space, opening. I am a shadow to everyone.
The heaviness no one can bear. I ring my invisible little bell. Leper!
beware. I am aware, but barely in words. The sound of my feet on the
snow. My flame guttering small. I want to get to the end and sleep.
There's a place I know, it can't be far from here. I have followed his
instructions to the letter. My master. It was all his idea: all I had to do
was live it. I shouldn't use the past tense, it's not over yet. I might just
have been talking to myself. I can feel the others - I only have to name
them - but they are figments really. Clothes I shed to this final one, alone
one, me. I have been lucky, I think. I know many who never got this
far. The knowledge eases the load, a little. Even if the whole thing turns
out to have been a total illusion, even if there is nothing but this, step
after step; and the rest all dreaming, visions that protected me from a
space I secretly could not bear; it was too large, too empty, too mysterious,
perhaps. I don't deny what I've said, but I remember strangely little of
it. And I have no desire to turn back the pages: I've wasted quite enough
time as it is. I know two things: I have a load to shed, to free my back,
to stretch my arms, to sing again and be glad. And I have come to meet
the master. The Shadow Master. I have come to ask him why, or perhaps
more appropriately *what*. What is this. This person. This infernal world.
I have a babel of questions. I shall probably forget all of them, and it

doesn't matter. I will hear what I need to hear. Perhaps I shall survive it, or not. I heard voices back there. I was being discussed. 'So why does he think he's come here? He doesn't belong here'. 'Perhaps he feels he has to bear its burden'. 'Or else he secretly likes it all in some way'. 'Certainly he has chosen to come here. Or has he?' 'I don't know, it's very dubious'. So what have I been doing? that's a long story. It began. I found myself repeatedly in a tunnel whenever I closed my eyes. As I began to share my experience, I realized it wasn't unique. Quite soon I realized everyone I spoke to knew exactly what I meant, whatever their reactions happened to be. I began to see we were all in it, or rather, continually going into it and coming out of it, rather as a diver goes down, surfaces, and then goes down again. I must say I never wanted to come here, anymore than you would want to spend your Christmas walking about outside in the snow being mistaken for a tramp. Let's say I experienced it as a duty. As a duty to becoming human. As a necessary journey without which the vision could only rest on a mixture of conjecture and thin air:

> Wings turn
> To fire and air
> But we of flesh
> Are flung back here

We may be angelic - at times - but we are not angels. Our task, somehow, is to live here, in the eye of the storm, on the edge of time itself. Depending on how you see it. Depending on how you're feeling. Depending on how much you can rise through your feelings and see. A lifetime of seeing. Depending on how much of it you can take on always knowing how limited your vision will be, that there will always be a piece which doesn't fit. There will always be you. And there will always be this imperfect workshop full of imperfect beings like us slowly learning and living the never ending story. It's not a matter of simple aquiescence. It goes much deeper than that. It's a matter of recognizing that everything which exists, like it or not, is part of the whole, and part of the truth. The question, maybe, becomes not how to solve it, but how to hold it. How to hold it and hold on and be here without falling to pieces under the colossal pressure of our times which demand we recognize, and for the first time, that we are all in it together, and all a part of each other. I came her to find out about that as well. And particularly, in what I loathed and feared most. To take the step, after years of waiting, of being prepared even though I was at least 50% ignorant of the process, to say yes to my shadow. And stand back, astonished and humiliated, and, what? realize that change is impossible without accepting what is. And in ourselves. Our world has a enormous skin to shed - already it is loosening, already the changes are taking place. We are being turned inside. We are being invited to become conscious, living beings. We are being invited to participate in something infinitely greater than ourselves, call it what you will; and there are enough names around for it. I have no name for it, because I don't know. But I am it: all it is is also in me, however lamentably unaware of it I also am, however continually I have to fall down and trip over to notice its undeniably manifest everywhere existence. This, if you like, is our mission. We all lead a religious life in the end - there is no other way to live. What was it she said? 'I said to the man who stood at the gate of the year: give me a light that I may tread safely into the unknown. And he replied: go out into the darkness and put thine hand into the Hand Of God. That shall be to thee better than light and safer than a known way'. There were signs everywhere, flashing themselves discreetly at me, as ever: saying come, come. And there was my fear. Fear I would go in and never come out. Fear I would go mad in the process. Fear I would lose my vision for ever. Fear I would cut myself off from all the sources of protection that have sustained me and cloaked me from the worst forms of astral possession and disintegration that cheerfully advertize themselves unknowingly across hundreds of cinema screens. I feared all that, and still I knew it was worse not to go than to go. I had to see if the light could survive hell fire, and if my light could outgrow my own fire. Perhaps I have had to burn myself out, I don't know. Perhaps this is part of the cleansing, the transparency. We have to live out somehow what is inside us to conceive of experiencing life differently to the hell it seems inescapably to be, and is, for so many of us in this valley. And now suddenly I recall him: that energy without which I wouldn't be here, even in this snow covered desert of England. And I am amazed at the exactness and accuracy with which it has all unfolded. I am amazed I had to do so little: only, to be truthful and persist in that, to believe that, for itself alone and without any promise or outcome. And then for the first time I experienced his power. I was sitting alone at night as its force began. It was dark and very strong. It filled my body, it breathed in my body. It felt as though something that had been in my head for years had loosened and was flowing down inside me, through my heart, my belly, my thighs and down to my feet. I felt I could lift the room up. I was black fire. I was him. I was the earth I was standing on. And for the first time in my life, I experienced what it is to feel fearless. Only a year before, soon before I was about to be brutally evicted from where I was living as a result of a disgusting and false allegation, I went into a pub on New Year's Eve half an hour before midnight. The bar was crowded and everyone was talking loudly in fancy dress. It was an ordinary pub in a small provincial village, but I had opened the door on it. There was a man dressed up in a Victorian suit and tophat, another as a rich Arab sheik, another in a wig like Danny La Rue. The clock struck, then the drink began to flow, and the music turned up. Appy noo yer! Appy noo yer! It was hell. Everyone was having fun, and it was hell. The balloons were coming down from the ceiling, Wham! was on the tape deck, and the whole thing began to pulsate like a German expressionist painting. In front of me, a woman in black stockings and suspenders was dancing with a fifteen year old kid who was gazing fixedly into her eyes and smoothing his hands up around her half exposed thighs. Someone bumped into me from behind, laughing uncontrollably. The music blared out of a speaker right beside me. The walls and faces began to close in. The woman was kneeling in front of me with her tongue hanging out. The boy was sweating over her back. The Victorian was grinning at them through his half glasses. The sheik was throwing handfuls of fake money up into the air. The boy came out of her and wiped himself off with a ten pound note. The sheik stepped forward and hitched up his gown to deafening applause. My stomach was churning. I began to go dizzy. I made for the door.

It was time to go.

Light not sweet, but strange.
Voice in the shadow.

16 parallel, simultaneous sections. Mapped conceptually. Unfolding ad lib. Format: each section dreamt as a tube journey. Quotation, dialogue, free verse and prose description intercut - conceived in the passage of language itself. A medley of voices and visual scintillae structured around the spiral shape of a black hole, reclosing upon itself and its self-characterizing contents. Genre: a ciné-poem-cum-fantasy, in which the author acts as disidentified, self-directing camera lens. Preferably read in situ, as experienced.

The necessary garments: boots
                        black Homburg hat
                        long grey winter coat
                        black shirt
                        black trousers
                        sweaters, scarf
                        mittens & thick socks

(and talismans: a simple wooden cross, a white unicorn, and a gold Cretan coin depicting the labarynth)

The marble, in close up. It is black. Slowly, as it turns, it becomes translucent green. A figure is walking in it across a snowscape. Piano music begins. Tracking shot of figure from behind, moving close up, then to shoulders and head, as before. Soundtrack of mixed piano and feet on snow.

Darkness. Sounds continue. His feet and breathing. Cut to deserted street he is walking up, towards an arch in the twilight. He passes through the arch, and pauses. Outline of landscaped space, with a lake on his right, ahead of him the thin strip of tarmac path, and, silhouetted in the distance, the rising walls and towers of the palace.

Walks ahead up the path. The silver lake water, and the cry of geese. Shot from above, his figure diminutive, walking up towards the reversed L of the path which then turns towards the palace itself. Pauses again. Looks ahead, at the next arch in which a single light is shining. Looks back at the way he has come. Reaches in his pocket, and pats it. Hesitates. Then walks forwards.

His steps. The dim lit arch ahead of him. It is now almost completely dark. Slowly the arch closens. He comes to it, pauses, and makes a gesture of drawing something down over his head and face. He buttons his coat fully, turning the collar up, and walks over the threshold, into the coaching yard. The echo of his feet off the walls, crunching over the gravel. The sound disturbs him. He softens his step, towards the arch in front of him, crossing, under the light, and emerging, to his left, briefly holding out his arm and gloved hand.

Silence. The palace façade rises in front of him, its windows all black except for one, over towards the entrance, behind which is a lit chandelier. He crosses towards it, his steps slow and rhythmic. Again, shot from above slowly panning down towards him as he closens to the huge pillared entrance, in front of which is a series of flat ascending steps. Again, touches his pocket, his hands by his side, his eyes looking towards the tall studded dark wood double door, either side of which are two iron knockers.

He walks up the steps, standing in front of the door, bracing his shoulders. Then he places his left hand on one of the knockers, his right on the other. He leans his head forward and closes his eyes. Then he begins to knock. The crashing sound breaking the silence. Then the sound cuts, as it echoes inside. Slow motion. His eyes still closed. Then the doors open inwards. He half stumbles towards them.

Darkness. He falls forwards. The image blurs. Sound of rushing wind. He lies face down. Above him, the wind rises in the smoke-like air, towards the dim outline of a cupola fifty feet above hime. The smoke darkens suggesting an enormously tall standing presence. Slowly, he turns as if in a trance over onto his back, his eyes flickering open, looking up. Camera from above. The wind begins to subside, and the smoke fades. He hears a voice, invisibly, from somewhere above him

'You have climbed by falling to the pit of the valley, welcome'. Slowly, he gets to his feet, and stands, with his hands in his pockets, his head tilted upwards.

'I have three things to show you'.

The Fantasy

Action. In an instant, the glass-tasselled chandelier is reillumined. He turns abruptly to his left towards the din of twenty or so voices talking above the clatter of knives and forks. It is the cast, having a feast. The long table, draped with a white cloth, has been laid for a full three course dinner with cut glass wineglasses and shining silver candelabra. It is laden with bowls of fruit and the remains of food.

He stands where he is, half-hidden in the shadow, looking across at them, silhouetted against them - Victorian, with his napkin tucked in at his collar; the blind man with his stick propped beside him, talking almost inaudibly to Private Jenkins, leaning forward in his chair; the puritan attentively making a note of several books the narrator, in his creased bow and tuxedo, is reccomending to him; the lovers, sitting speechlessly facing one another, touching each other's fingertips and gazing into each other's eyes, while the joker in his court fool's costume entertains a pair of serious male communists in combat jackets who stare at him open mouthed...and so on, round the arrangement of drawn back chairs, including a selection of specially invited 'old friends', and several beautiful anonymous women who emanate a strange dream-like glow...to the head of the table, which is vacant, its place still set in front of a large carved wooden-backed chair. Then one by one, they begin to fall silent. Their faces turn. The silence spreads. The joker's bells tinkle as he leans across and clicks his fingers loudly, once, between the lovers. Briefly, they all look at each other. One of the women raises her finger softly to her lips and holds it there.

They stand, silently, looking over at him. Then they start walking slowly towards him.

He steps gradually backwards, out of the light, as they closen in loose file, their faces set in anticipation.

He stops. They stop. They form a circle around him. He begins moving round on the spot, from foot to foot, acknowledging each of them in turn and holding their eyes.

And then they step forwards one by one in his gaze as he stands still...and as they closen, their figures blur, lighten, and begin to dissolve through each specific gesture they each make to him, as he glimpses his own face in theirs, reflected back, and in his body as it blends with each of theirs, through his eyes...as they pass into him.

Finally, he is alone. Then, he moves back towards the table, as the half empty glasses and plates vanish. He comes round to the head, draws back the chair, and sits, leaning forwards to pour himself some red wine from the decanter.

The Dream

The glass empty, his fingers still holding its stem, his head slowly leans and slumps forward, moving the plate he has just eaten off vaguely out of the way to one side. He lays his head down sideways in the crook of his arm. One by one, the candles begin to flicker, lower, and snuff out.

He hears a voice. It is a woman's, talking to him in his mind. His hand moves from his side, smoothing up his shirt to his heart, where it rests. 'That's where John came in. I found the harlot in me. I needed her. I remember, we went to the theatre. I'd booked the tickets and the table afterwards. I engineered the whole thing. It was the same when we went away for our weekends. We arrived at the pub with half an hour before dinner, and went straight upstairs to our room. I was daring him. I stood there, as he glanced out of the window, smiling the way she smiles as I unzipped my skirt. I was claiming myself back, you see. It wasn't about love: it was her. He complied, and even if he didn't understand, he was kind. The truth is, I was furious deep inside, furious I had been let down all those years. And now? I can own her. She's mine, inside me. She loves my body. She loves me through me. Do you see?' His eyes closed, his mouth begins to part. His hand stirs, rises, and a deep drawn out sigh heaves out of him. His lips begin to move. He is talking in his sleep, his voice pronounced and slurred. 'If you want to come through... this time...you must stand up...exactly as you are'.

Blackout. Then a dim greyish blue light slowly begins to brighten, alongside a faint high note, at first almost imperceptible, then loudening, increasingly, into a continuous zinging hum...as from between his shoulder blades a whitish airy substance emerges and gathers, forming a replica of his own body, and linked to it from just beneath his stomach by a length of silver cord.

Music: at first distant, then closening. The light around the stand-

148

ing naked figure starts to move and vibrate like a slowed-down strobe. Then the figure starts moving away towards the sound, into the shadow beyond the table where the light filters through from, and into the empty space where he begins to dance.

Music in me, through all of me, echoing its beat from my head down into my legs and feet, up my thighs, and down into my arms, wrists, hands, fingertips. Then the ground beneath me began to move, to turn, to rotate; to whirl as I began to whirl, with my arms outstretched, looking down, down towards my stomach, feeling something taut and witheld beginning to loosen; and, at the same time, inside me, a clear detached core of stillness that was watching me dance as I danced, unmoving, waiting, calmly witnessing. Then the ground turned black, beneath me, spiralling, bottomless, seeping up through the soles of my feet and filling me. Then I could see nothing, could only feel the blackness, and my stomach still stirring and invisibly expanding. Somewhere above all this I heard my mind coolly evaluating me, matter-of-factly listing my least desirable qualities: I am cold, I am lustful, I am selfish, I am competitive, I am aggressive, I am arrogant, I am charming, I am manipulative, and at the end of each phrase I heard myself saying 'and I can choose not to be', and each time, I sensed the energy behind each word becoming lighter, lighter and more powerful, as the sounds of the words fell away like husks. I heard a man's voice saying 'You are guilty of being human. You are forgiven'.

Then my stomach opened. It slit down, between my legs, and up, around my heart and along the length of my arms, and as I leant back I saw figures rising up out of me, out of the blackness, their features etched in black light: a satyr, a salesman, a Royal Marine, a businessman, a black magician, a lead singer, an adolescent and an aristocrat - and the satyr showed me his penis, the salesman his mask, the marine his physique, the businessman his wallet, the magician his power, the singer his throat, the adolescent his heart and the lord his loneliness - and as I saw them each as they really were, they began to become transparent; and they moved up into my mind and out from the sides of my head as my dancing slowed, the music began to fade, as the ground steadied step by step and returned. I looked down at my body and saw it had grown denser...and I watched the outlines of bones forming and hardening...veins, blood, and skin tissue, skin, hair...pants, shirt, socks, trousers, shoes, sweaters, scarf and coat: turning in the silence to lift, swing and re-shoulder its tense weight, standing, head bowed. And then the sadness, enormous, unbearable, as it swept down. And I said 'I am dead. I have accomplished nothing. Let me go. It hurts too much to live this. Don't you know? Is this what I have to come back to? I'm lost, it's too big, I can't hold it, there's too much of it, it's too far down, and it won't stop, it won't ever stop'.

And woke, holding my heart. And whispered...surrender, I'm through...just tell me the truth.

The Reality

I sat facing you on one of those black sofa chairs, as myself, nothing more, in my worn black winter clothes: and told you the way I had come to this ending. Godknows, I said, I might be given nothing and told to go away, but I just want the truth, however small it is, or I will never become what I am. I have come this far, and frankly, I can take anything. I don't know what happens to him. I got him up the path through the dark to those double doors, that's all I know. I'm a grounded bird in a human skin trying to talk human and wishing I could fly. It's been a long trip for one so unborn. And I want to be born.

So I closed my eyes, saw myself, and walked back up there. Yes, I said, I'm afraid of this. You asked me what my fear needed from me, and I answered, all I am wearing, even the weight of it, the humiliation. This is it: this meeting, moment, climax. I need everything I've got. But as I said that (and somehow, passed through the doors without either knocking or trying to open them), I found myself standing in what felt like more of a church than a palace, and, pilgrim as I was...I began to grow...I began to rise, taller and taller up into the hooded daylight silence until I was forty feet high, with my head and shoulders reaching up into the curving dome. I stood there in my soul, with my eyes closed, holding back a sudden urge to cry, as I looked down at the tiny human figure that was me there beneath him, looking up at what he had come after all this way to meet; and I knew then finally what I had to give him, out of the darkness, out of the soft enclosed shell flesh: the thing itself, the ending, the full stop: a deep rich black pearl.

I held it down gently to him, as it shrank from its cannon ball size in the lined palm of my hand. With my eyes still closed, I reached forward and down, as he stepped hesitantly to receive it. Then I felt myself descending, coming down towards him, coming gradually down into him: half way between me and him, his story I was born to tell and he to live out.

And then gently, you brough me back and out, to feel my feet on the ground and my eyes waiting to open, as a great silence came over me of a kind I have never known before...and then I heard you asking me to bring the pearl out with me, and I did, and through the blur of my naked eyes I looked down at it, and him, lying there curled up; as I held my other hand open, like the oyster, open and breathing in a shaft of early spring sunlight that shone out from behind the grey mass of cloud, slanting its ray of warmth through the window.

Pilgrim, rest. This is the place, this is the time. The long night is breaking. The dawn is coming, the sap is turning, the buds are growing. And the first bird is about to sing -

the calm place

Alba and aubade, everything goes

I walk out to find this place

I was a child and still am, and now
forty four years later, I can see you, in your uniform
walking into Assisi at dawn
the pink light rising on the buildings
the desert and the death behind you
the massed white cross graves
held in the same calm inexplicable light
after all you'd been through, to feel like that
the weariness of those beside you
in silent communion

The calm that breathes everywhere
the calm that is finally being itself

At the last outpost beyond all belief
I stand with you on this slowly awakening earth
With the city behind me

the saddened black abandoned windows of the house
and the flat where love ended, vacant, For Sale
the memory as if frozen, and the snow unbroken

And back it goes, the calm, back to the heart
released from its pain, its torrent of feeling
the stamp of each day that slowly consumes it
in the humanness it is here for

I walked out among the twilit trees in ignorance
it was enough to lean against one and close my eyes
with my feet by its roots and my head soothed leafwards
where the branches stirred and whispered *enough*

Or that time driving up through Shropshire,
with the sun huge as it set, no longer blinding
but strangely vulnerable - and a glider
swooping down over the packed silhouetted woods to a halt,
and the handglider with his pterodactyl wings
dipping down and out of sight
over the trees and the combed furrowed earth
the car easy in gear
the windscreen like an open book

The opening held up like a negative

The air calm as a blank page all around me

A man sitting by the river, thinking
A voice saying 'I am going under a mountain'
A voice saying 'This is where I am - this moment'
A voice saying 'The mud and the light and I are one'
A voice saying: paint these pages over and over
in thin streaks of bright rainbow

My voice saying *begin*)

Sources

The text, as I assume is obvious to anyone reading it, is a dense multifaceted tissue of voices and quotations which revolve around the slowly emerging central thread as it is narrated. They derive from both personal and collective sources over what essentially constitutes the last hundred years, although, as is implied, the Valley itself is as old as history. Aside from friends, lovers, relatives, aquaintances and chance encounters among the anonymous (of whom the unnamed author is also a part), I see those rather better known names that follow as what they were and are for me - fellow faces, and familiar or not, contemporaries nevertheless - tunnel pilgrims, mental travellers who spoke and still speak of the Shadow we still find ourselves in, and through which we are all incompletely journeying.

Written sources in quotation marks (see note that follows) in order of appearance are:

epigraphs: D.H. Lawrence, from 'The Ship Of Death', Arthur Koestler from an interview, Libby Houston from 'Childe Roland Takes On The Dark Tower One More Time', and Dr Moody as cited.

intro: 'un dereglement...' from Arthur Rimbaud, in a letter.

Victorian: 'Implacable November...' from Charles Dickens' *Bleak House*; 'Come into the garden...' from Alfred Lord Tennyson's *Maud*; till with the refluent dance...' from Charles Tennyson-Turner's 'A Country Dance'; 'So I returned...' from James Thompson (B.V.)'s 'The City Of Dreadful Night'; and phrases that follow with ref. to Thomas Hardy's 'The Darkling Thrush' and 'The Voice'.

the blind man: combined phrases (from 'I wasn't ready for it'), from Wyndham Lewis' *The Sea-Mists of Winter*, and Henry Green's *Blindness*; 'In numerous cultures...' from George Steiner's *In Bluebeard's Castle*; 'In the Valley Of The Blind...' from a notebook by Andrew Harrison; and 'as a deeper blindness...' ibid. Henry Green.

war: 'And Germany's place...' from James Joll's *Europe Since 1870*; 'Oh oh oh what a lovely war' from the musical; 'Its a new sensation' from Roxy Music's 'Do The Strand'; 'On a moonlit night...' from Lt. Col. C.L. Proudfoot's 'A Warrior's Welcome' (*A Soldier's Song*); 'The soldier's cocks...' from Rimbaud (*Complete Works*, transl. by Paul Schmidt); 'When Tyson...' from Eric Williams M.C.'s *The Tunnel*; 'I don't want a holiday...' from The Sex Pistols' 'Holidays In The Sun'; and 'shantih shantih shantih' from T.S. Eliot's *The Waste Land*.

Cedric: *This Is The Modern World* by The Jam.

in body city: 'His imagination...' et seq. from George Lamartine's *Cabaret Splendide*; 'If the body farts...' from Samuel Beckett; 'The grave's a fine...' from Andrew Marvell's 'To His Coy Mistress'; 'Finally I pulled it out...' et seq. from Henry Miller's *Quiet Days In Clichy; L'Immortelle* by Alain Robbe-Grillet; 'Peggy and I...' and quotes which follow from *Forum* (the journal for human relations).

tube text: 'Its a whole world...' ref. Jeremy Silver's *Travelling Dangerously*; 'Face without me' and 'The world is everything...' ibid. Andrew Harrison; 'distracted from distraction...' from Eliot's *Four Quartets*; *The Journal Of Albion Moonlight* by Kenneth Patchen; 'Between the conception...' from Eliot's 'The Hollow Men'; 'All pain vanished' et seq. from testimonies quoted by Dr Moody (as before).

in a poor country: 'Sharply the menacing...' et seq. from George Orwell's *Keep The Aspidistra Flying*; 'No one loves you...' from Bessie Smith's song of that title; *The Wonderful And Frightening World Of The Fall* by The Fall; 'Power To The People' by John Lennon; 'Come brothers and sisters...' from Bob Dylan's 'The Times They Are A-Changing'; and *Let The Power Fall* by Robert Fripp.

love: 'Where do I begin...' from a popular 50's song; 'Listen to the wind...' from Fleetwood Mac's 'The Chain'; 'I never was attached...' from Percy Bysshe Shelley's Epipsychidion'; 'Love oh love oh careless love' from a Popular English Song; 'Je suis le tenebreux' from Gerard Du Nerval's 'El Deschudado'; the vortex itself...' from Theodore Schwenk's *Sensitive Chaos*; ref. and quote from Andre Breton's *Nadja*; 'Let us abolish...' from Roland Barthes' *Camera Lucida*; 'No one here can love...' from a Popular English Song; 'Look, we have...' by Lawrence; 'There is no escape...' et seq. quoted in H.V. Guenther's *The Tantric Way Of Life; Oh Les Beaux Jours (Happy Days)* by Beckett; 'Love', he said: from Andrei Tarkovsky at a press interview; 'ye that have...', from Christ's sayings; 'And yea though I walk...' (*and see title*) from Psalm 23; 'The opening gets narrower...' from a short story by Emile Zola; 'For in love we surrender...' from Susan Griffin's *Made From This Earth*; and 'I will try your vanishing...' from Brian Patten's 'Vanishing Trick'.

the joker: title from an abandoned film script (with Mike Mitchell).

the counterforce: 'Men Of England...' from Shelley's 'Song To The Men Of England', and refrains ('arise, arise') from 'The Mask Of Anarchy'; 'ye are many' et seq. (and Paris, May '68 graffitti) quoted in George Woodcock's *The Anarchist Reader*; 'the enormous tragedy of the dream/in the peasant's bent shoulders' from Ezra Pound's Canto LXXIV; 'you can't shoot a fascist...' from Orwell; combined quotes in caps from the RCP manifesto *Preparing For Power* (et seq., and *Socialist Worker*); 'In Russia...' from Vladimir Borisov in *The Daily Mail*; 'It would be nicer...' from E.P. Thompson's *Protest And Survive*; 'The constant preparations for war...' from David Lea & Peter Marshall's *Gwynedd: Peace Or Nuclear War?*; quotes in caps contd. and with ref. to *City Limits; Veronika Voss* by Werner Fassbinder; 'The stuff you're writing...' from Dylan, in an interview; 'Contempt for politics...' from Michael Hamburger's *The Truth Of Poetry*; 'they blamed on God...' from Albert Camus' *The Rebel*; 'There's a natural mystic...' from Bob Marley's 'Natural Mystic'; 'The only possibility...' from Joseph Beuys; ref. 'Protecting Life' by Cheryl Moskowitz; ref, 'this is the revolution...' from Alan Jackson's 'Reasons For The Work'; and 'neither Left nor Right..' from Johan Quanjer (ed. *New Humanity*).

what the voices said: 'All sense of the soul's life rapture...' from Algernon Swinburne; 'The dark I cannot name...' from Jorge Luis Borges; 'We are in the asshole of the '80's...' from Taggart Deike; 'I spit on life...' from Blaise Cendrars' *Ocean Letters*; 'till the darkness cracked...' ref. Doris Lessing's 'Through The Tunnel'; and 'from the other side...' from Alan Jackson, in a letter. The rest is personal.

livid darkness: 'It was during Advent...' from C.G. Jung's *Memories, Dreams, Reflections* (with Anelia Jaffé); 'all words...' from Peter Handke's *A Sorrow Beyond Dreams*; 'Thus he speaks...' from Vergil's *Aeneid* (bk. 6) transl. by Brodie (et seq.); 'If you want to know...' from Italo Calvino's *Invisible Cities*; 'The city favours...' from Malcolm Lowry's *Lunar Caustic*; 'To the centre of the city...' from Joy Division's 'shadowplay'; 'O Thou vampire...' from The Scarlet Woman, in Aleister Crowley's *Diary Of A Drug Fiend*; et seq; 'Stab your demoniac...' ibid. Crowley; 'Where do you think...' from Longmans' pamphlet series *What Would You Have Done?*; 'Dark tunnel...' from Sylvia Plath's 'Three Women'; 'Hey man...' and following phrases from *The Evening Standard* and *The Daily Mirror*; 'You're right...' from *Octopussy*; and 'This is the end...' from Jim Morrison/The Doors' 'The End'.

death: 'Be not fond...' from *The Tibetan Book Of The Dead*, transl. by W.Y. Evans-Wentz; 'Lighten our...' from the *Book Of Common Prayer*; 'A slip...' from the museum at Dunwich, Suffolk; 'The lonely one...' from Hermann Hesse; 'I must grasp...' from Phillippe Jaccottet's *Seedtime*; gravestone captions from *A Small Book Of Grave Humour*, and 'We learn...' from Henrik Ibsen's *When We Dead Awaken*.

the unknown; 'I know that I hung...' from Hávamál's 'The Words Of The High One'; 'I then decided...' from Oliver Fox, quoted in Celia Green's *Lucid Dreams*; 'But one forgets...' from Beckett's *The Unnameable*, and 'I said to the man who stood at the gate of the year...' from Marie Louise Haskins.

the calm place: is empty

A note on punctuation

Because of the complexity inherent in the nature of this text, I have evolved what I hope is a consistent method of punctuation which points to its different layers, in so far as it is possible to seperate them out from what is, at every stage, a lateral, nonlinear continuum symbolized throughout by a continually moving spiral.

The differentiation works as follows:

i. the inner voice of the main narrative thread appears in a series of parentheses, and in small lower case verse form. The last parenthesis which opens in **love** remains open right until the end.

ii. sub or 'fantasy' personalities, fragments of mimicry, parody, prose, and journal entry appear without inverted commas, as they are heard (or written) inside the mind. All the main 'characters' and third person references to 'I' are of this kind as they finally form the emerging figure that is 'I' (the pilgrim).

iii. written quotations and fragments of exteriorized dialogue (inside and out) appear in inverted commas.

iv. descriptive action, in which fragments of film instruction are included, appear in ordinary face.

v. stage instructions and emphatic speech appear in italics; advertisements and expostulary headings in caps. Song quotations appear in inverted commas, italicized; and titles appear in upper and lower case, also italicized.

Dark before the dawn,
Stretched to the light's edge:
The green light ahead, and the black
Road that has led him here -

Pilgrim in the valley of shadow
A man near the century's turning
Brought to his knees by the roadside

Black clothes and shrunken aura
Black wind breathing between his eyes
And the weight of what has been
Still clouding his brain:
'God dammit, I've been in hell'
The unowned fear, violence and shame
The sheer body, the hairy hoarse
Stench he had to climb over
And fall to the end of his mind through
The dark that comes before the dawn
The darkest hour, when along the path
Came the God Of Darkness Himself
With the pilgrim's skull in his hand

As he kneeled, and keeled over
And the weight opened in front of him
The poisoned river gouted out
He vomited paper and black blood
Slush of maggot, fungus and skin
Pulling the length of it
Out of his stomach -
The hell of the body without soul,
The hell of the heart without trust,
The hell of the mind without hope

In the dark before the dawn
See his tiny head and huge feet
See the weight strapped all over him
Pumped like a blood pressure tourniquet,
See his body immured in a mould of rock
See his clenched fist and bared teeth
His mouth opening, the hiss of his whisper
Croaking out life! life!

And he is so near, but he can't see
He can't speak for the swabs in his mouth
He can't hear for the deafening sound
Of the tunnel imploding around him
Of the unknown sky he is opening
Of the face he has seen as his own
To come to this

Chrysalis, in the stillness
Webbed and woven around him
Threaded with earth, grass and leaf-vein
Hung in a garden shed out of the rain
Surrounded by hands as the green flame
Gutters and stirs

In the dark before the dawn
On the eve of the equinox:
Cloud covered moon and stars
In a dark room, only trusting
The left hand's uncurling, unfolding
The strange half-formed writing
That it knows and I don't

And would sit, or stand
Waiting in this moment
Willing nothing, not even
The spread rainbow-winged flight
Before I am ready

To be born into the heart
Of the Angel Of Life.

DIVINATIONS

for Carole, in love & faith

'The terrible vision of eternal energy of good or evil, of man made in the image of a creative God, of the power of the spirit as it works within him to his destruction or to his redemption - these visions we release from the dungeons of the heart, and we release them in fear and awe as well as in love. The descent into the self is the most dangerous journey man can take, for to know the Self, the Self that dwells within one's self and encompasses one's self on every hand, is to arouse a hidden life of unforeseeable, unknowable creative possibilities. It is a discovery of the spark that becomes the fire that can quicken or consume. It is the terrible vision of the God in whom all things become manifest.

This is the journey, this the return, through which we may learn to know - to realize inwardly - that 'the only way to ascend unto God is to descend into ourself', and the only way to manifest him in our small individual lives is to 'return to the most human, nothing less'

- Frances Wickes

prelude

'When I go back into the ground, into the depths, into the wellspring of the Godhead, no one will ask me whence I came or whither I went. No one missed me: God passes away'

- Meister Eckhart

THE MIST

1

Morning blue and bright on the village,
A warmth brought birds; picking at bread bits, on the lawn.
And then the cars gradually in, as the Stores opened
And the florist's - as the van
Brought in the papers, in passing.
Then men, drilling the road - distant as summer
And so, as the day slowly eased out of true
In the vague afternoon...
As the van came again - so soon, to take the post away;
Mist stole in too, softening the roofs, parting the houses
And drawing out the sea road...as if by suggestion,
A late car's flaring exhaust flame;
An uncertain perspective.

To walk down

Had to

Walk down
                    towards the sea

to be with its quietude.

Easily, knowing the way so well
Steps in warm, worn-out clothes
                                        invisibly

making a silent vow, to no one.

Past the last house
At the edge of night

- remember a death, going towards it
  strong as tall, seeing down
  on him driven, back
  against a wall...

An elderly woman calling at her little dog
Mig-non! peering over a torch
As a moped headlight wobbles round her

And fades
        vanishing, as a light
        goes out in a window

pauses, standing

before the short path

whited, insubstantial

- a soundless excitement
                dropped, like a match.

The end of a known world:
A South Coast beach.

sat by an old winch
and a scraggy tamarisk

waiting, what for

as glad if nothing would happen.

Didn't need a thing
But an empty thought

to be, wrapped

low in the mist
        on the damp pebbles.

It's hard to be silent.

Mist
    beach
        composed
            sea-sound

growing
      out
         into
            itself;

- no voice

to be heard
but the way
a word
comes to you.

Waving it away

but no wings for it to fly

so on, it stays; it sits

Like you.

You want to see: mist.
You want the mist, to look
Through it

Watching the beat
of your eyes

but inside
still repeating
that slogan yourself,
to no purpose.

Released -
                a man down the pebbles

on the sand
                still walking - into the sea; wading out

                        up to the knees

And another, sitting
observing him

lucky man, he's nearer the mist than I

an another beside him

Released
To a pitch

Like a fantasy
                    bits   of a limbo body
                    dislimned   a-flicker

shapes in the mist
voices in the water
in front of your face

as you know yourself

on the island of this place

to be: unreal.

2

Back where you are -

both silence and the mist
stay, unbroken

- in a jolt.

quiet, be so

quiet to silence

and listen outside of the grip

of yourself:

thought adds

thought as it opens

in you; the creases of a paper dart

a paper boat

each phrase

become meaning glimpsed

through the wording's floating blur

to where its
unfolding
intuits a
language as yet

unknown to you

   - could you

  but could you become one

with its signal:

and live at its
depth, brought in you,
here

filtered inside of you
in the body

become air

become channel to its
presence that is

Spirit
         quickening, under

your hair
         shivering
across your back -

for a moment, as the moon

floods sky

mist
       and the mind's sea -

and this-as-it
comes to you
is what you come to

3

A closing of eyes.

Getting there
Where you were
Takes so long

till at last you arrive
by closing your eyes

and how strong the silence out of you;
how delicate the silence within you

now the mist has brought you
to this place

especially to disown you.

And as you turn and walk away
And turn to look again
And as you turn and walk away,

It is forever.

———

a poem, hidden
deep within a poem
till somewhere, sometime
there was that poem

that you missed entirely

Angmering-on-Sea
1980

MEMORY

My nose had bled, inexplicably
for several hours, on and off
and when it stopped, finally
I went out to do the shopping -
I remember hurrying
past the flower-girl
in through the rusty wrought iron gates,
past the closing stalls -
the men in green overalls
lugging topheavy crates
of cabbages and aubergines;
and into the butcher's
standing in the queue
watching one of them
sweeping up the sawdust
while another beat out a side of veal:
and now the mother
with her short ash-blonde hair
big eyes and bobbing earrings, holding up
her purse, close, clumsily to open it
her body heavy
under her tight clothes
as she stands half over the pushchair
feet apart -
and her baby begins to stare at me
his eyes lush blue
and mouth closed, calm
at the hacking
only four feet behind him,
his slow clear gaze reaching through mine
into this stillness of my seeing him
as his mother moves
apologizing, sliding her
full bag down her arm,
opening her purse, taking
out a crumpled fiver -
as I reached back in my pocket
for a rag of tissue,
sniffing, as I blinked away, staunching it
and still those blue unwavering eyes

and he won't smile
and he won't stop looking:
as the cleaver
crunches through some awkward bone.

unrevised

A MOONSTONE

A glint of blue on faded velvet -
At the centre of my mind:
And the crowded jostling Market fading,
And me with it. I can't remember why
I was there, hanging around, not looking
For anything. And then it found me -
Bent close to it, filling my eyes
With its clear cloudless blue expanse,
A dome of sky high above a ripening harvest field,
Reaching right through me where I could not enter
Its pure, translucent reflection.

1982

elemental

'There is no indifference to the world outside us when we come to the inner soul-world. We feel ourselves completely grown together, and woven into one with that which here may be called the world. Its activities are actually felt streaming through our own being. There is no sharp boundary line between an inner and an outer world. The whole environment belongs to the observing soul just as our two physical hands belong to our physical head'

- Rudolf Steiner

'In orgasm, we share the force that moves the stars'

- Starhawk

WIND

Gathering.
Walked, high up, in the trees' waving.
Splintering the softened late summer sunlight,
Now, again, deeper into the wood's green shadow -

Earth wind rising, its invisible wave
As we slip our feet grip treading the mud-path petering out:

Stream gushing out from under a bank swells as it sinks
Underground, and the river, far below
Glistening, meanders over the patchworked fields; as it builds

In the silence and begins
The trees' tops quivering downwards, their trunks
Vaulting glimpsed up whole in their each and then all
Of-them-coming-alive - wind

Crashing through, deafening, tugging your hair back
And your face, amazed, as it spreads around our backs, breathes
In for the next blast the crinkled leaves cling on moth-like and
Flow past in uncatchable armfuls -

Blown, our arms reached wide and hand-held, silenced
As your breath escapes you; and the trees' roots shiver the earth
On them as they sway the sky high clear and cloudless circling
Tall in us wind swooping and cradling

And then giant again, drunk, the trees knowing it
The trees dancing it, and we are as water, willingly
Let's run, you say it with your eyes and forehead tranced, loosening
Us, sung silenced into the back of the brain's

Old earth-love open-mouthed swallowing us into this strongest -
Of-all-sense, that is as it has always been, belonging us, through
This wrenched-out exile; dissolving, here, and came with you, here -

in Her I vanish every dead thought into

NAKED

In the house of the body, a ghost to himself
Sits, quietly, and then the sound slowly entering him
Twilight in the falling light hovering imperceptibly
Through the large window-frame, watching
The tree's leaves beginning to redden

As it steals up from the house's foundation
A tangled rustling, disturbing and edging him into its
Feeling spreading gently, tingling, over his body
And beneath his clothes, caressed
And at first, surprised

As his eyes see him strange in this skin skein
Not knowing where the sound is coming from, and then
Reminding him - as it catches - the two of them
Downstairs fucking tug him into his senses
All at once as she cries out

Uh uh, close on his chest, and opening his heart
As it beats up drawn into their rhythmn, uh, panting
In slow motion mouth-to-mouth and he is silent, it is
Her sound its muffled whisper loudening as she takes
Him up under her fingers

Their bodies rippling as it closens between them
And fills up the room and the space of him drawn out
As if in standing, his clothes flake from him as he steps
Into this body that is him, standing here, hearing her
Twilight-skinned belly taut and heaving

Her power, released, the spittle fire shape of her
Rising behind her flung head and closed eyes high as high
As it can and then uh uh uh she is it is so beautiful
Nothing can stop it now from coming -
And down through the static hazy grey air

The rain, at last soothing and unclenching him
Outside the window and into its cool calm liquid light
Flooding behind your eyes seeing nothing but its streaming
Deeper and brighter than blood in this depth of you

Splayed at one together

And in the sound dreamt into, its echo come into him
With no word left in his head but this one word
Coming back and lingering, unbroken, between us
Where we are naked and with nothing left but it
Having nothing left but its spirit to surrender to

As the grass gleams with rain and each tiny second ticks
As another leaf drifts from the young crab-apple tree
As their aftermath beckons me
To you, and to be

always ready
to fall-all

brought down
to seed

in the body we secretly
long to be reborn

RETURNING

Listen now, lie down standing up.
On the bridge my steps stop.
It is the step that leads to this -

Suspended, fleshed
On wet winter rooted earth
                              on the spot

where the river tumbles and opens
under the road.

White ethereal mist.
Seen through trees.
Inside the eyes. Islanded

here, raining. Alone with river
Close eyes and slowly all becoming one river,
pausing
              to tread forward
                              and walk with it, in me

Where in the heart of its shimmering roar, it is holding
Its hiddenness, openly

And flow-following, out, to beyond me

wading into the ground

DUMB

All ear
All quiet
All calm of face

reborn. And dying, in one. Perpetual moment. In the space of this

that would speak, and in speaking - cannot. Can only in this silence

deepen, undistorted
to sink, level
into you your
deep self your
openmost

unwritten-on-page. Essentially. Close to, but unconfined; resting with the
arms folded, and face turned inwards and unruffled

into its deep pool presence of soft grey twilight; sitting in a darkening room.
Feel the blood now slowingly being bathed in its own flow, in its own
way; and follow, as its balm steals over the body muscle by muscle still
as its pores open; and at the entrance to the sky between your eyes

and to the roots of the hairs on your head
where I imagine placing my hand
and to the tip of each uncut
crescent fingernail

I say be dumb, be undone. This is strength. Not to jerk up awake and
go over to switch on the light - but to break

through this deaf crazy wound-up depthless wording strung from your
shoulders like wires...that water washed away, that your clothes covered
you again renewed; and sat, and suddenly lost all sense of habitual
movement

and stayed with it   went down with the sun   let eyes fall

let limbs refuse to move   shirt loose, bare hands & feet   letting

this strange gentleness mould around...

outside, the cars sea distance   Saturday Night

ebbing away from here

and the breath   almost   completely   unmoving

in this open awakened and clear-seeing being, blanket-wrapped - and the rest fallen away, the rest gone to a vanishing point of light. The screen you switched off as the feeling started. And behind the old man in his smiling wrinkled brown skin, a petal falls from a bunch of flowers arranged in a vase; as he spreads out his hands, and smiles, and the frame stills, your finger presses the switch - and you look into the emptying screen

into the plenitude of this

richness that will rise

to bear you out from within

your drop of deathless ocean

> look up at the sky
> and down into the earth
> in you -
> and if you know it
> it shall no longer
> be in words, but in what
> words once were

- it is unspoken.

THE RIDDLE

for Peter Wilberg

Secret, self
And itself protecting:

In what the echo
From your saying
Off the silence has
To tell your Self

In what was once
God but which now talks
Back - beyond the void -
In your inner light to you;

And what, and where am I?

Speaking it as spoken -

As I become you.

EARTHED

for Jackie

Twilight winter mist, blending
Field-and-wood silhouette -
Neon town a floating slick of orange stars;
And the silence - the last car gone from the place
Down the wet lane; and the hut here, with its hearth-fire
Shut in shadow, turned over to the night
As the words you are reading blur, and then illegibly
Dark as the sky's deep cloudedness, covering
The moon still hidden

And the Stones like strange broken teeth
Bleached by three thousand seasons of standing -
The soft, worn limestone pitted and ringed, moving
Motionlessly round: still, as that time is still here
Where we stand - still, and yet gone, forgotten, memoryless
The witch's elder tree a damp hacked stump, and the soldiers
Who followed the king in this shrunken fleeting myth
Are scattered; harvest upon harvest ago, rusted into loam
Numb voiceless after-images - and us too,
Dreamt in this, at one in the living web of earth

Pacing the slow circle huddled round against the cold
And touching each stone's shiver
On us watery ghost-flesh, the quiet shadow
Of your almost invisible face under a white beret -
Passing by your light wordless smile
As you wander out and in among the nearby trees

Leaving it to me: going round, once more, alive-alone
Drawn towards the centre that is a trodden square of mud
Worn open by the thousands who have shared this moment
And entered here:

Crouch down
The eyes closed
To empty the mind's
White light
Back deep into

The earth

Spread the palms out flat
Half-bent, half-knelt - and as the moon brightened
Into its half-grown glow

Lay the forehead down
On the mud's cool, the grass-dew
Soothed speechless, clear dark and imageless
Giving over of me through it spontaneously...

Stood back up; and the muffled echo of a church bell,
A mile off, fades; as this holds, in its calm

all-embracing
                unburdening
                            ending.

WATER

Sea without light,
Home of the body.

Ran to you in flames and rushed in
Ran out of words and rushed into you -
And I still call it love, which means
I am making this journey to your otherness, woman.

Quicksilver bird of air
And bird with ash in its mouth in a dry dry place;
Parched shadow figure that can no longer go on
Without this sense of you under my skin
Walking along the dark street like a stream
Above this mother dark, and below, its depth
Surrounding and outliving this death
Nurtured in you and your thousand faces.

I carry your face in me and it is moonlight
Over the sea where the dead man floats on his back
In a long dreamless sleep without thought or memory
The blinding heat erased from his mind, the light
That raged until it burnt his brain out, gone down
And his empty eyes looking up at the moon
And his body slowly ebbing back to life,
Half-sees the shore on the other side closening
As he walks now, dripping, onto the sand...

Comes to, in her room, as his glass is refilled
And the wine running over him dry and him stone
As we talk, the four of us, until you decide to dance
Spontaneously at the sight of your own body
Curving and stretching to the music you turn up:
While he sits in the armchair and watches you
As her silence draws me in to dance, letting
The change come naturally bringing us to this
My steps moving up out of my mind into here
Finding you slowly edging your way closer
Till we began to dance together as we were
Hardly knowing each other's names and no matter
There was nothing we could talk about better than this,

Listening to the music as it began to move in you
Following each nuance of body that you made
And that you let the music make, your half-closed eyes
And arms raised letting the sound flow through you
As I danced with the dancer in you, touching her
Freed from myself as you were from yours
Without wondering if we were going to fuck
Or what time the last tube went or anything -
Nodding lightly goodbye, as the music ended.

Gladdened, walking away then, alone with the night
Off the road and out of sight among the trees
And over the hill to where my steps simply took me,
Lying down on a bench beside the glistening water
The sound of it coming through the weir for a long time
As the empty bottle slipped away and rolled
Sitting up, as a few words came back
From the beginning as I spoke them to myself
In a voice he came here to find himself saying:

I downward
I darken
I become water.

INTO THE DEPTH

for Carole

Of this
Speechless closeness.
You cannot misunderstand it
If you want it to mean what it is -
I can tell - although
The words stick in my mouth, they
Won't come out; even
Inside, to me.

So I let them go.
I let all of me that I know go.
Forefinger, motioning my own lips to close
And then inching to slowly open out to yours, friend;
That you have filled my slight body up
To the brim, with your being, and it is this -
Kiss - as we cross over

Where our faces darken as one in the same space,
Tongue over tongue and into the depth
Of a darkness starred and streaked with flickers
Of breathing light -

Sky we wander and mouth this making love in
One unspoken language we are being spoken in -
Falters, searching for a true way for itself out here:
And at the same time as I turn away back to your mouth
I know it will not, where it finally begins,
Need to be written. So this is to say, kiss
And in your heart go through this - tear out this page

And take it if it has reached you -
Because only the closeness can know, can ever know -
How deep the well-shaft with its water we drank

leads down to the seed

we were born to live

IN THE MYSTERY

Sea's edge.

Distant roar of the wind, taken back
With the tide. Sea's edge -
Where the sun has sunk...
Crackling, steamy hiss of damp wood
And dark air as the earth moist, moving
Under huge black clouds -

Promontory of grey lichen-covered rock,
Shadows of tall trees and wind-blown gorse
Level to the draining sand echoing birds
Their twilight song brimming around a rim
Of silence, out to where the sea mist reaches in,
And brings the mountains down, blurring the houses
Into dots of flickering uncertain light
Buoyed on a sea of air, until the cloud clears
Leaving the estuary rippling under a spray of spread stars.

Slip down,
Treading near the water
Where the voice is whispering
Pause here: and make a preparation.
Gathering wood and kindling, bent
Blowing flame to fire and curling smoke
To make a sacrifice, of self
To this element.
This dark.

The forest waits, to be turned to, inland
Through the dark trees to the forest within
Alive with streams spilling up over the paths
And breathing the wind in the dark where her voice
Holds the place full of secret openings, under the leaves
Where I push this seed of us deep into the mind's earth.
And I am dumb with feeling her through my body,
As she unravels and unfolds me. You kiss me, you undress me.

Goddess, I have come to meet you in this forest
I have drunk wine and I have stayed silent

My eyes have emptied me out and turned inward
Into this dark of you. I have let my body tell me
What to do, to be deepened into this heart...

And as I lie down awake on the ground and feel it turning,
Through the whole of my body being grounded here:
Stretched out with the earth moving silently into me
Seeing my nakedness streaked over with earth
The rain dripping onto my forehead and closed eyes,
Your hand slowly smoothing down the line of my skin
As you come to me in water, as water, as we merge

Now the forest opens as I speak your name
At one in our thoughts across this distance
Walking through the darkness with you inside me,
Seeing you in your dream as you saw yourself
Standing in your woman's armour and bone horns
At the centre of your being become light
Where you will enter and become what you are
Your mouth healed from its cry of despair
My love, your strength

Now the forest opens and you open around me
I come into this depth of you and am made essential
Elementally my own self in surrender -
Mouth open, legs open
Where the trees become sheer and part
And between them

    it pours out pure

IN THE TEMPLE OF SUN

for Alison & Francis

'Lord of mercy most loving,
He maketh to live intelligent beings,
Opener of every eye,
Proceeding from the firmament.'

- Egyptian 'Hymn To The Sun'

'My heart, my mother;
My heart, my mother!
My heart of transformations'

- Egyptian *Book Of the Dead*

'Only that which can destroy itself is truly alive...'

- C.G. Jung

With hair the colour of cropped harvest the sun shadow came.

And all the world was one sea
Where I lie down, inert, floating

Far out...on a lilo

On the salt sea dead still
Dead blue sea surface,
Laid to rest, turning
Slowly round, breathing

The slow bobbing pulse of the water

The eel-dark sea urchin deep below
The deep deep deep simplicity
At the depth of the light

its naked blinding eye

Sun, feed me, sun secrete me
To sleep back to the beginning, the New Making

this sowing slowly bursting
the seed of my sun voice
out through my skull sky

Eye of Varuna, eye of Ahuramazda
Eye of Ra, eye of Zeus-Dione
Eye of Dionysus and Apollo
Eye of Light and lightening dark
Eye of Marduk and eye of Tiamat
Eye of Ch'ien and eye of Kun
Eye of Yin-and-Yang
In Yin,

He stands, lifting up his hands;
Eye of Sihai, and the sun comes through his fingers,
The Rising One, numbs as his body becomes utter

And wholly heart thought out into the sky's space,

His body surrendered, limb from limb

Half under the surface
From where I stand on the shore, facing a waste of sand

Eye of Gaia...

All Sun All Seeing All Sensing
That is us in each spark of seeing, soul, source
As of this sensuous skin-touched air
Brought out and up and outside into
The light on the water's

electric calm candescence

Ripening born out of its dense dark hollow
Hole, that was night, slept, huddling under rocks
Hid under the ground, crawled famished
From each day's fought-for survival trance
From each day's dance of death in the mind

Sun up out of nothing,
Inexhaustibly inside you
You who came from lightness,
Come again to our eyes

. . .

I love you love we love sun. Here on the shore, as the days pass and wheel, almost motionless.

Beach-scene laid out, heat on pebble-white, bleached, pumice-dry, from either side of the bay, spread.

Bodies bodies bodies spread, spaced, sleeping and playing on the dream edge; held in this fluid unsaid multiple of thoughts being thought in each head, drawn down by the sun, silenced by the sun, surfacing, to chatter and then fall off...above this depth, this parallel space the eyes begin to blink inward to

standing inside of me

imagelessly, to begin with, simply the dazzle, that is impenetrable, as the sun itself is made to be: uneasy of access

and as ever how to begin?
at this entrance, threshold that everything visible is standing at under the sun -

begin, to unwind, to undress to the light now as strained white skin begins to redden and tan in the dark my skin my only clothing on the way to that stark delicious nakedness inside

that is not him
that is not here yet
that is beyond him

that thought self, like his water-self
swum out into dissolvingly
into the sea, the sound and the lap of it
throbs moving down under the heat
the hot whirr of noonday cicadas drumming
and the distant humming of an outboard motor
entangled in voices, shouts and splashes;

...surfacing now in him, in his eyes, between watching and being in among the Children Of The Sun fooling around in petalos and canoes, snorkelling & splashing & swimming all day long, slouching over at the taverna drinking beer and licking at ice lollies doing nothing about anything or anywhere in the world, blanked out, unconscious

but that child
that memory-child I lost behind a blaze of light flickered for a moment and was gone again leaving me holding a large pebble he had painted a huge yellow sun on with the light pouring out of its mouth -

and all day
across the great suspended
clockface of the sky, the blue pause
the far shore, drifting towards, beckoning:

...and breathes back again onto this beach, across from the White House

where the 11 a.m. tourist boats come in distracting all of us out of our
heat trance gazing over at the swarthy Greek sailor men dancing their ritual
routine as the hands clap and the deckload cheers, then they stream in
and out again, shipped off leaning over the edges of the boat blaring out
bouzouki music roaring out over a chorus of drunken male voices

that the untroubled silence
absorbs, in the wake
from the stern...

piecing inwards, closening
                              to read this

blank light page
                    his eye is turning

his hands among
                    the sea's work, a piece

of frosted glass
                    triggers beside a scrap

of curiously
            weightless bone -

thought-darts of swallow shadows
                                    dipping-

-and-curving speed
                    between him talking

and it
        soundlessly tracing
                            these pocked inscriptions

joining up the dots
                    into lines

shaping a figure
with a bow bent
arched back -

The king is approaching the temple
That the sun shadows into a five-pointed star,
And the king is nothing and the king is alone
Without consort, his kingdom, his soul
Laid bare, his capitol abandoned
To the people

And all under the Aten, one sun
Spirit that has darkened
That has been lost

Now he returns through his dethroning
Through this death of himself
De-frocked, uncrowned, as if erased
Become a beggar, a leper
Become naked

He comes for initiation
He comes as he was born, knowing nothing
And he is old as stone, he is ancient
Symbol of a condition called 'sun'
When the spirit sang in the body
And what is now esoteric was magic

Was the moment reaching beyond bounds
Into what is now unknown again
Lost echo lost voice

Him on his knees, dreaming him
Digging down under the grey
Into what his hands his skin knows
Into what he knows now he is alone,
He can remember he can connect it
The dream with the body

Come back into the body
His spirit is walking in

And him stone-face, alone-face
Heavy and clumsy-human
Beside these silver fish shallows,
Their rising from the sand
Their bellies glinting

As part of the light, raining down

And in the wake of each wave
Butterflies brilliantly pick along

tremblingly

- each one of us alone in the living day,
In the transient time it takes
Out here in the open
To ask the unanswerable
But what any life is answering
In reaching the height
Of its own aloneness

Alone, gone away from you, I am leaving you
As the gap still further closens towards me and closes

In the empty frame he is standing in

Facing a waste of sand -

And if this is love it is the old fire burning,
As old as the mind burning to be itself
And be surpassed, this time

I have my innocence

That is my ignorance I must suffer

To hear the voice

To take the step into desert

Where there is nothing but oneself
To begin to go beyond...

and become this journey begun in a dream
a white seed   become   a whole world

between two worlds

the far shore

in the early morning mist

beyond the body

in the body

this shore and that one, this one

the sea between

two worlds

in each wave...

packs all he has, in a rucksack; leaving himself there, and you there sun-
bathing fast asleep...and turning nods goodbye goodbye in his mind to
the goddess of the beach at worship in her glittering emerald slip-string
bikini, smoothing herself langourously over in oil, stretched out, her hair
tied up in an artificial flower beside he, Roma, in his red trunks and pitch
dark ciné-shades, the pair of them arranging and rearranging themselves
to perfection

and that suave unsmiling instructor on his windsurfing board its yellow
Bic sail idly catching the breeze he skims effortlessly into, leaning out and
looking back expressionlessly at the hoi polloi on the beach, as he begins
to merge with the distance and the cloudless blue
and the shimmering bay rising

at either side above the water
each cypress standing tall
and singly reaching, and beyond

where I must go

to the unknown country

Desert of air, waste of water.

Dark, formless mist.

Waiting for the sunrise -
Shining rose-bright
On every living thing
Its eye lights up,

Born through the sun's eye
To speak the thought
Of each thing's name -
As it word-worlds in your being
Its single endlessly fleeting gaze
Of stillness moving, deep
Into dark empty space

Before the sun was

The light must travel through

this darkness
at its own depth

. . .

down to the river
frail flow of a dark street
City megalithic
in dying neon, sun dying
down the end of Sunset Street:

now figures, shadowy, move towards the Western Gate: all eyes and mine,
alert, automatically, on the lookout...it's late...don't stop for anyone...you
never know...keep moving...eyes front...close down, wrap yourself
around...this is how it is...how We The Living live here

scenario as the sound cuts
the screen flickers and the screen is hard
it fills with blood

he falls back through plate glass
into your clenched mind
into your brain's blood
like blotting paper

hurrying down with it wrapped round your head
pass down this flight of stained littered steps
arms-and-legs rhythmn running along
round and down the stairway's
dusty blackened metal
breeze-smell of tramp's piss
buskers' lament echoing

shade of cypress and of yew
wet smell of graveyard ivy
moans, sobs, ambiguous cries
calling on the coming night
countless faces, herding disjunct
trapped voices imprisoned and diminished
there is no light no light

inferno kids hunched over fruit machines
jacking up on electric violence
spilling out the eye, crazy as a pinball
shot round and flung from second to second
zombies revving into the breaking light
vultures' wings spreading and clawing
this is the Book Of The Dead

this is how it is, this is normal
so sit with arms folded and legs crossed
around your only flame of light
sunk where you are going to
the Dark Heart the Drowning Pool
all aboard the funeral train
all on board the ghost train

faces fed by disease and cruelty
vox clamavi, Lord we are ugly
her cold white stare stopped me dead
as she drained my energy and drank it
so stay close, chrysalis
let the voice guide listening in

follow him, him with the jackal's head

Horus, battered sceptre in hand, bright seeds in your pocket...begin to scatter them, now it's getting darker

passing through a high wall, where another gate opens...and far ahead, in the sound of of your own echoing steps

slides the sun-bark, the dream bark the dream-of-strength bark: the great ship moving ahead, its prow scudding through the black water as the tall figures stand and chant and the song surrounds them as they move on towards the Snake

at the midpoint of night

the Snake's body, a ship's length, with three giant human heads, and hawk's wings, beating above the water, the hiss of whispering voices and the glimmer of eyes around it, as the eyes become faces, snarling sputtering hatred, their taunts ringing off the thin shield around you, spat at, and punched in a flurry of insane laughter as they swarm around the victim, pushing and kicking, tearing at his white miasmic form

but still the steersman steers on, unblinking, his eyes like mine turned inward as the ship moves into the fire where they tilt and tip back from the side of it, screaming in agony, their arms in the air, their heads aflame, as his frantic strokes closen, panting, in an exhausted crawl, towards the stern, rising sheer and unclimbable, grabs on to the top of the rudder with one hand the head hung floating

as the ship moves silently into the Nether World and the Snake follows it under the black water, and the air is mogodon-heavy, the figures steel themselves to stay awake in the deathly calm as the Snake rises and hurls itself against the ship's side, thundering across it and sliding back, its scales glistening, the teeth in the smiling heads drawn wide, the wings showering droplets of water - and again, as the whole ship shudders in the Snake's grip

the hand's grasp weakening

the water pulling back

and the dim almost inaudible sound...of a woman's voice...as the mind lets go entirely...lips murmuring, begging

Isis, release us
come into my heart
and hold me there

and her voice dizzy inside him his eyes rolling and then closing as the
body is dragged up out of the teeming infested water

. . .

begins to wake
past hoping for anything

around the ship
the dawn beacons blazing
dispersing the air

now the darkness is breaking
the darkness is a vast shed skin
drifting away

clambers to his feet, and looks out
hair blown back by a fresh cool wind
the blackening-blue sea lightening
and everywhere the air clearing;
it's over

rubbing his eyes as a white dove
flies up alone into the primal blue sky

and the Great Egg on the water
breaks the new morning world open

as the burning sun's disc begins to rise
the river reaches the ocean and streams out

...and in me this welling of dry tears, and smiling, walking outside to be
with it

as the sun now at zenith moving through the white of a cloud, a white
yolk a white hole above my beached body

begins to re-emerge
                    at its edges
shimmers,
          melts,

begins
        to whirl
              above the body's navel;

(as he lies with his feet drawn up - clasped - touching his head

                    where
                she stands
                above him)

3

Sand. Haze. Sun   entirely fills the sky.

sulphur blaze

there is no horizon

- to the centre
  I go -

out beyond the city walls. Timeless in desert time. Walks, barefoot, broken
staff.

broken, the spell of his own power

him renouncing him

walks. To reach depth. Rescue. Her in him. Find her. It is far. Unspeakably.
In the bruise that he is. And it all is.

the way his eyes must see

walks, across the dead surface. Hollowed out. Hollow I. That this space
is. And trusts it. And has no other choice. The way his eyes…dim seeing
necessity at his core.

It is just enough strength, not a drop extra; rationed, like water.

Here all is fire, truly, that he may be. Or - he may simply die en route.
There is no guarantee. None at all.

and no voice but
this eye all around him

sees: on the ground in the sand in front of him a pile of collapsing,
shrunken little balloons melting down into skulls, multicoloured, mouths
parted, sigh, wordless air, as his face speaks

this is the border of silence: if you have nothing, you may pass

beyond them, and their rapidly dissolving features, a large piece of faded
and tangled material bears the insignia of a rainbow out of which the col-

ours are visibly draining

into the colourless sky
skull sky sun sky

and wants to turn back, but he cannot. A touch, briefly on his shoulder.
And then a tap. Go on. Smiles, maddened. Floods behind his face to all
that he is and has been. Bowed forward. But - strange joy, is it?

nothing that is real survives this sun

invoking him dead. All his human ghost. Of an intense human life. Con-
fused chiaroscuro. Starts parting layer by layer. These memories. Of all
his beginnings. And unbeginnings. He knows, and they don't, only *it's*
beginning matters. Only.

this straw in the drowning air
pool, whirls; dizzy-thirstful

pictures him to himself now -

inescapably. Image after image. Undesirably. But at the same time like
looking at someone, something else, this him, this I. That is being eased
beyond...nothing can survive

this light in the mind. In the eye. And so begins to re-see. How it was,
is - and then the gap, the unknown unfulfilled unbegun

horizon he moves towards
from centre empty, from centre
no longer adequately edge

grown too accustomed. How it feels. And thus this. Must tell. And in the
voice that body becomes - the only chance. That spirit articulates, this.
Tension. To have this willed on him. An ambiguous compliment. Smiles,
lop-sided. Laughs, and then looks away. Moods flash the whole range
of him. And evaporate. And must empty out

to the core, the bare
unadorned spark
if he is to become
free of being

to enact the voice

his reverberates, hallucinates old cave-thrown flame shadows

'first contemplate thine own illusion', of everything, as it clings in its filmic memory-wrapped package of contradictions, superimposed, echoing. Silence. Silence, but him not. Him not ready. Him full of noise. Him full of the noise of him human.

The contents. Day after day. His steps take years. He stops to crap. Snail trail, bowel, belly-trail thought-trail. Piss trail. In invisible ink. Ink, the sun warms and words and takes back into its air

wandering, to himself, visibly; as what he sees, thinks, appears in this shimmering air out in front of him, colouring the shadow cast ahead of him his steps walk one after another into...his own mind

in the dead of love now haunted by images all weaving themselves into one face which like his own he cannot see...a tangle of hair and the blur of soft skin in close-up, all of it, these years of longing

and still his love remains unanswered and unloveable, without a place to be...a road, a ream of tiny crosses marking the way, a road littered with holes, and he sees them, lovers that have failed and fallen lying in each hole naked and exhausted, apart, their bodies closed beyond touching

and still the one love which drove him on moves through all it has touched in its passion till there is nothing left to touch, to speak, to say

and still the wound that is the heart of him of this opens as far as the eyes can see...and in its clear sky he is trying to see them, loving, the voice in them, circling each other as they speak and stand close, surrounding the shape of each other, calmed; their eyes open

and then the hole opening
swamping the image in darkness
the hole become a mouth
feeding off them, insatiably
shouting, shrieking hysterically
lost to all they know

sacrificed to destruction

and so wanders, dressed in black, soaked in sweat, swinging a half-empty bottle of wine and the taste grown sour, all of it, overwhelmed, burning in him, this black sun, and this light that strikes out between his eyes, sore, bloodshot, his body hungry, angry, and all the rage he has been blazes out in front of him, scalding the sand in the shadow, and the stone on his back, the ruck-sack frame bites

and somewhere still
the child's face
its voice, insistently
and the sound of a child crying
beaten, rises up terribly

as if his clothes were on fire, as the hell races back through him leaving him shouting out loud all you mud-locked and meat-eyed clever clever made-up monkey puppets spouting slick slime surface death fuck musk-fart clockwork manoeuvring manipulating spiritless frigid arid, soul-sick, soul-sucking, every violent epithet he can think of banging through him, unleashed, every last drop of disillusioned bitterness punches out through his clenched fist catching the side of his own face, staggers, on the edge of this helplessly blind void that lies behind it all, falls over, blood on his fist, blood on his cheek, crouches, his body hunched, opening his hand stuck to the handle of a knife he tries to shake off, and cannot, the pity, the pathos of it

and still on the other side from where his wet tear-stained face runs

he stands, his body no longer bent, but standing, and reaching out his hands, giving everything he has from him into this heart, and asking, and demanding, nothing, it is enough, this...he knows it, only to give and help ressurrect

at this fallen edge of day
turning twilight among the trees
standing by still water
and then looking down
over the flickering cityscape

for a moment, and then it lurches again, deep in him, beyond him, beyond his control, the fear draining down his spine the drumming again in his ears the sand blown against his face, caking it

sees: an hour-glass framing the sky, voice rushing as its grains fall, his eyes sheer horrified up the sand like a wall and collapse back, as the voices louden, in every language and then rising up in the centre, a huge figure, its bones picked clean its arms folded over a greatcoat, its eyeless eyes staring…as he becomes ant, becomes insect, crushed, smashed legs wings and antennae

and his own death, finally   suspended in it,   spinning round, crashing in his ears, his arms stretched   wider and wider   as if letting the world out of him,   letting it go, longing to find the sky rushing under him and jump -

and then the ground
coming back, steadying, returning
hangs on deliberately, simply
to the action of each step

as the sky returns clear and imageless, blank space all around, and draws on his mind, but no, nothing there, just his steps

desert desert desert

and all of him - image, that's all, letting it all be said and done with, leaving it waiting for him in its unimagineable and still and always invisible

presence, for less then a second, and less than that…in the brackish water he scoops into his hands and into his mouth, kneeling at the oasis with its dying brown palm trees

before the last stretch -

lightens, come back into his body, him watching him, his voice trying to rise and then falling back down his throat, into his stomach, the pain there beginning to lift under his hand, the wound closing

the mind at last beginning to stop

stops, scanning the limit of what he can see, must reach, must get across it, his body insists…and finds it suddenly easier going, his feet following the path of a dried-up river bed that seems to be widening

as he slowly zig zags from side to side of it

his strength so much less now, felt faint, felt it coming, stoops, and is sick, dumb animal sick; and wishes the river were water to wash him away, and sniffs the heat for the smell of salt the sea, but not yet

smiles, ash around his mouth, wipes it; drunk on sun, dazed crazed idiot smile flaking; and what clothing he has left hangs ragged over deep brown skin and dim blue eyes, the body so thin and defenceless, watches it moving, poor fucked thing, and his thoughts breaking up immediately vanishing, traceless, like type sunk in white, unthinkable thoughts, buzzing, waves them away, unthinkable and irrelevant, of no use now

he asked to be brought through them and beyond them, and he is, he is -

and the mind void
is being prepared
in his unknowing

only: to live, through this. No other desire. No other expectation. Nothing. And his throat a lump, his brain sunk, and his name he tries to pronounce, to whisper, like a whisper calling him

My name is My name is I am not going to die

now no water left

and no food since when

can't remember, can't hardly can walk, only the will left, a thin steel wire running the taut length of him, keep his eyes vague focus, keeps him forward crawling,

through a forest of smooth dead white trees, trunks, branches he snaps and grips onto behind his eyes, and then gone, his hands touch the bare sand...pulls himself on his belly, rests, and then pulls again; slides down, rolls over, stops, turns over, and then crawls, on again...

his eyes almost shut

half-sees ahead of him

a camel, a mirage, finally mocking him, but struggles, to his feet, somehow, blinks his eyes, but it is still there, standing, waiting, staggers over, reaches out his hand, and yes, rough hair the hump he clambers onto, and falls back, and the third time makes it up...and tips forward grasping its neck, weakly digs his heels in, and again as the ground begins to move under him, rocking him

breathes, a trickle of moisture still in his mouth, sucks at it, his head throb-
bing, opens his eyes a fraction, the dry mud again, but all around him
now...covered in bones, scattered ribs and limbs, laid out, everywhere,
crawling, one by one, trying to reach forward

and then gone

can hardly hold on, now it fades inside him and sputters out, to nothing,
nothing he can any longer recognize, become a mere thing-corpse-carcass
being drawn on, half gone into the camel's body, feeling its moving begin-
ning to loosen something in him, slack and motionless, stirring something
that feels no pain, a numbness he feels is also him, but not of his mind,
outside his mind

inexplicably

it begins to pull him, approaching, ripples, circling rushing soundlessly

a waterfall of air

now where

the heat pours

its light down through him

falling, plunged

through him shapeless

down down down

into the brightness

- and then it
broke:

slowly
       awoke
             breathing...

all around him

...liquid, amoebic light.

A hovering black dot.

white sky

white silence

white covering

substance around his skin and eyes. Like a membrane.

Light walls, curved above and beneath him floating, turning round and round. Stirs, bathing in it. Cool. Strange dawn light. Sea calm

strength, where from

and yet: in this thing him. Gently through him. Begins to feel around him ...towards...touches shell.

Floats back, closes eyes. Rests, very slowly, to wake, only that knowing. Now reaches hand, through shell, peels it back...and the first glimmer of light outside is the same colour

and the heat gone

as he slides out, and stands, from crouching curled up; and can, easily, can even walk. A step. Pauses. Looks ahead, still hazy, and...is this

the temple

and am I?

intact. Body complete. Naked. Feeling over him, and around him

touches air

4

An olive tree marks the spot
Where like a pillar stood
The Sacred Oak.

It is said that the first temples were simply groves of trees...

nearby runs a streams,
its cool plashing
liquid through the air

I stop, digging carefully with a spatula

among fragments of forgotten dreams

as part of a dolphin mosaic begins to rise. Beside it, a few feet away, a
fallen column drum. And then a series of boundary stones

scattered scored lines

marking the enclosure.

- what must have been the Telesterion

the map an uncertain reconstruction

dating chips of limestone,
divining in stone

a way
        what way
                in?

to these
silent, impenetrable ruins

                    .   .   .

in our mind.

- in your heart, ignorant and hesitating. Voice in me.

Walk back slowly, turn round, and try again

A stretch of Doric columns reach directly in front of me. An avenue of battered stone lions.

a welter of clues that catch the light,
and fade...peter out

like sand through the fingers.

Close your eyes

begin to drift
                    round and round

the ledges
            of an amphitheatre

moving
        down
                towards the centre:

where she stands
                headless stone
                        & V-shaped wings outstretched

- touches ground.

Touches the ground with the flat of his palms and his forehead

> *Great Goddess, mistress*
> *Of forest and mountain*

guide me.
Imagine me.

and lies down

First, he goes to the spring. And stands in it, his skin ringing with the suddenness of it; braces his body and then relaxes and lets it wash down over him, lifting his feet, his arms, tipping back his head as the water runs over his hair into his eyes over his forehead.

And then stands in the light, drying; his head back, his eyes closed now.

The light behind his eyes brightens, becoming translucent, brilliant blood red.

Walks, now it's time. Step by step. Along the Sacred Way...the pale chiton wrapped loosely around him, feeling the movement of his feet along the line

as the columns of the stoa
begin to converge

in the distance

in a single
shaft of light,
coloured the same
as him, washed skin
and semi-transparent
covering drawing him
                        towards it

as inside it
              between his eyes

a figure
          begins to emerge:

as he closens, and quickens

A woman.

he stops

She is standing in front of an altar. He is lying on it, his body, laid out; immobile and ashen. He starts, as she turns to it, and closes the eyelids with the tips of two of her fingers...and beckons him, in.

I am dead. Threshold. This heaviness. Head swimming, a thick sensation spreading back through me. Dead. But? must be inside somewhere, can still feel, dimly, the lightness

tries to open eyes but can't

It is like trying to lift stone. Sleep swimming. Eyes a sea. Can't think, no more. No more sun. All sun burnt out. Abandoned. Left behind. I am all I am, here, in its hands. What to do, to say? and why this body I don't want this body back take it from me

tries again to open eyes. They open, blink open. And it is dark, pitch black. Blind. No -

Be calm. Sleep.

Her voice. No words. Not in words, but in light

She says: if I surrender

...feel out towards the edges of...this stone-slab, but softer than stone; clay-like. Face down. In the posture of sleep. Trying to turn the body over. Can see nothing

only light if eyes
are kept closed,

it must be night

sunless, washed-up, shore of cool sand

...stands. Out of himself. Keeping mind completely still. One movement. Turn your body over and raise your hands. *Now.*

And then he sinks back again, his hands folded loosely over his groin. Blanks out. Completely. For a few seconds. Then his eyes slowly open, and he stands haggard. In his body. The chiton is briskly replaced. Then all sense of her vanishes.

.   .   .

In front of me, an oil lamp is burning. Beside the lamp is an entrance, as if to a tunnel. Steps move ahead down it...a rustling of cloth...and the sound of bare feet. Pause. Dark inside here. And cold. Dank. Body shivers, trembles.

The lamp flickers behind me. Something bat-like flits

a hand very lightly touches my shoulder

:in, come on. Stomach tugs, resisting. Legs weaken, as if shrinking. A warm breath moves across my face. My mouth moistens. And then it warms

in me, lingering and building, this longing, again, urging it, closer, deep
in this darkness, crawling now

and suddenly enveloped in softness, and in the brain, opening out, floral,
flushing warmth as mouth touches

and sucks the sweetness, draining in, the body come back, filling up, run-
ning through him, alive, wants to cry out

Mother...

and the god, seated
surrounded by light
staff in hand, Ascelpius
his face leaning forward
smiled, and listened

and in me began to gently
draw me away

and her face beside his

clouded in the dream-light, and then faded into the dark. I found myself
naked again and covered with warm smears of earth that were streaked
across me from head to foot.

Heal this now. Be seperate.

She is all over the earth, as she was scattered.

I touch my skin, and it is good, good to be in it

You have not taken enough care of this. It is stupid.

shamed

her laughter

burns, like a slap. And releases. A smile, the head bent. Come on now.

The ground steepens
                        his steps go down...

5

I have come to sleep in your temple.

Come into my dream now.

I have no gold
To throw in your fountain...
I hang my whole body as I am,
Standing here, on the walls
That I touch with my hands.

- falls,

sol nigredo

...and slides the rest of the way, as if down a chute. Rushing light, concentrated, in reverse. Does not attempt to hold on. The smell of the air abruptly familiar...burdened like a busy street, lurid brightness, clothed in flesh and glass; moving, endlessly, into the past...up there, on the surface...exposed transparency he walked through, on the way here...through his own...our own...mind-myth.

Beneath the crust of a rotting Civilization, beneath a reality which has no reality left - from which, his own death. Dead king, dead novice...burnt through white heat hell...sol albedo, purgation of a mind...become bared, and willingly.

In the temple of sun the sacrific is self

and thought, to her. Anima. Luna. Impasse. Between the dead patriarch and the new man. And it is far. Into lost feeling...voice...sliding, darkness, falling. Into what the body knows...into what the mythless man-body must himself give birth, to this spirit, through the crucible of the psyche itself. Dead psyche, crucified butterfly

must chrysalis through death and re-emerge, must intuit the journey and can only

between beyond the eyes

falling, falling through this limbo of blank air

null body and void mind. I have no history, but what is not. Not me. Not I. Godless, I have come to your temple. To this

abyss

come into my dream now

. . .

It starts with the sound of a heart beating. And the sound completely filling the space of him, loud, defiant. Frightening him...but as he listens and it draws him in, he gently begins to nod

This sound, deeper than yourself. Beating on. Beneath you. Open your eyes now

does so, and comes to. Moves back on his hands. He is staring at a huge skull, cracked in half, from the top of the nose to the bottom of the cranium. He is trying to focus on it. But it blurs, confusing him

This death's head is yours

staring back, toothless. And the heartbeat loudens again, and pulses, in side him. He reaches his finger down, and feels it, under his navel where it presses up...and then gradually subsides

as he leans back, on the rough and uneven ground. He looks forward, his head between his hands, as the dull ache in it holds him

Beneath him, just visible
                  is a deep gully:

and through it runs
the River Of Fire
there is no crossing
but by foot,
             wrapped around
                        eyes closed
                                 heads bent

into the pit's depth...

his heart sinks

and with what strength
to crawl the other way
back, up the well-shaft?

Up above, it is worse. The passage ascends and then stops, blocked by
rock. A plug of granite. The light filtering through its edges

as he pushes, and pulls

but it won't give. Thrown back again and again from it...exhausted. And
utterly depressed. Deadlocked. Wordless.

This rock cannot be barged through. There is no short cut...so

back to the well-shaft
stairs half buried in stone dust
garbage and residual echoes in his head...

as it was
in the river
where he sang
on fire,

as the material fragmented

inscriptions
                    smoked on the walls
                                    graffitti & genitalia

at first descends -

in a crowd of meaningless dream images,
in a string of chemical reactions cancelling themselves out,
in this accumulated weight of blind statistical facts piled
in books stacked in computers and microfiche

The Man-made Machine's
                    abstract excretia

- tears at the fabric
he struggles above,
his head pounding
his wrists and hands

covered in words

'and from this descent come up deeper,
 come fully from the limit of yourself'

his ghost returned momentarily
to the whole of the life it had
as he heaved himself

step by step

beginning to recede with each
step up, towards the light

dreaming of a light
all around and surrounding
I still cannot enter

. . .

Lamplight. Beside a bowl.

A milky broth. He drinks it gratefully. It tastes honey-like.

Beside it, another bowl. Containing water. He washes the dust off himself,
and his smudged white face.

Then: a pair of scissors. He remembers. Cut my hair. Its blond streaks
fall, cropped. Then his face again. The dirtiest part of him. And as he begins
to rub it

his mouth opens
and his eyes, his forehead
opening wider and wider

until he can step through

Now shed now shed now shed the mask of mind

. . .

...dense tissue depth. Walks, with his eyes closed. The light judders, as
if walking inside him. And the light has eyes, myriad eyes, emerging and

receding...and moving round amongst brightening, shifting colours

and the eyes are seeing into him

and they touch his skin

and his eyes are among these eyes; but his eyes do not move, they stare, opened

while the eyes pass round his, weaving

and the chiton falls from him...

I am your mirror

again, her voice speaks. Come close now. You are among us. Her voice echoes 'us'. The eyes become tiny points of light, still moving, and then growing, enlarging
globular, as the pattern
moves, inside them

and as the light
softly brightens
their voices begin to hum
breath-lengths of a single note:

> Aphrodite, Pelagia, Anadyomene, Dione
> Ouranos, Pandemos, Kallipygos, Morphos
> Genetyllis, Ambologera
>
> Melainia, Melainia
> Aphrodite Hetaira
> Melainia Melainia
> Aphrodite Porne
>
> Andr-o-phon-os
> Andr-o-phon-os
>
> she upon the graves,
> she upon the graves.

I see you have brought your desert with you.

They all stop. Her voice sinks into him.

I am your mirror, your mirror. Are you willing to suffer to learn?

His head down, his voice catching, he says: I have.

You have suffered, but you have not seen. We will see.

Cast the circle!

dimly, their shadows cross to the four corners. One of them swings a censer. The smoke gives off a sweet jasmin smell. She stands, tall in the centre, with something wrapped around her neck and onto her shoulders.

It is a snake. They begin to chant:

> Is-is, Ast-arte, Di-a-na
> He-c-ate, De-me-ter, Ka-li
> Inan-na
>
> Her name cannot be spoken
> Her face was not forgotten
> Her power is to open
> Her promise can never be broken
>
> Is-is, Ast-arte, Di-a-na
> He-c-ate, De-me-ter, Ka-li
> Inan-na
>
> She is the moon
> She is the earth-light in the dark
> She is the bringer of harvest
> She brings the rain
> She moves the earth
> And she is ocean,
> She is the dance
>
> Mistress of mysteries
>
> She opens the grave
> And unwraps him dead
> Mistress of mysteries
>
> Kore, she dances him
> Nemesis, she suffers him
> Kali, she destroys him

Mistress of mysteries

She resurrects him

They sing the last verse twice, and then each of the women speaks a line each. Their voices move through his skin. He begins to watch himself, listening, behind his closed eyes. The Priestess speaks the last line...as his eyes open and he finds himself straightening up from his knees, his hands held loosely together, touching, the fingers pointed out, his wrists on his chest. His mouth begins to open as eyes briefly stare into his, and he blinks with their strength, feels it coming in through his eyes. She takes his hands and parts them. They fall, open and then rest by his side:

Come into the circle. You have come this far. So be here, now.

Are you afraid? he tries, for a moment, to look into those eyes. Her voice closens

I have been with you, and I am where you must return. Come in now.

Eat this. The taste of it immediately enters his mouth. It is dry and bitter, and it spreads in him, calming him.

I speak to your silence. Your word-self has gone. You have only feeling left. Be free to feel. The circle is holding you.

Then, as her voice deepens, she sings, and the women join her raising their hands above their heads where they move and sway

See him
Touch him
Deepen him
Release him

See us
Touch us
Entrance us
And dance us

Show him
And know him
Dissolve him
And change him

Cleanse his death
From him

That he may
Learn the meaning
Of darkness
So he can return
In the heart
Of your love

See him, now
Touch him
Trance us
Dance him,
Deepen him -
Release him -

Release him

Tears, one by one, well and run down his face. He cannot resist them.
His mouth puckers, his body shakes. It seems to come from inside his
throat, this crying, he has not cried like this before, so completely without
reason and recall. They watch him, contented. The Priestess nods

It is good. Let it.

She breathes deeply, once, and then slowly breathes out. The tears run
over his hands, face he tries weakly to hide. But he can't. He wants to cry.

Pity through him in this falling
Goddess, open his heart, this dry wound
Out into a flower, a flower of blood

He sees it, moving inwards, as the petals fall leaving a tiny closed dew-
covered bud which begins to open

Then his face clears, and his tears fade.

He is naked. He is ready.

Now you must be conscious. Watch yourself feeling. Conceal nothing.
It is a matter between you and your eyes.

Step forward, your body will follow. Now, open -

Sunlight fills the air, dazzling, but without heat. A shelf of rock extends in front of him, by the sea's edge. As it clears, he sees her lying there where the rock begins to slope down; her hands stretched out in front of her naked body, raised on both elbows, her fair sun-bleached hair swept forward over her face; her back tautened behind her shoulders and her feet arched, toes touching the rock; and beneath her, the sea breaks completely still...

He holds his breath back. Her beauty suffuses him.

Hello. She doesn't move.

Aphrodite. She says nothing. A light breeze ruffles her hair.

He gazes at her, her back turned, quite unaware of his presence.

He finds himself saying, his voice strange to him, his voice, but not his: I am out of reach. I am touched only by what I am. I do not need you. I am intact. I have entered you. And I have survived you.

The image trembles in him. He cannot enter it. He wants to look away, but cannot. There is so much he wants to say to her, but there is nothing to say. His nakedness burns, and it is not only his own nakedness.

You are a man. Consider. Look at yourself looking at me. That man is also in you. Admit him.

You see an image in your mind, full of your own desire. You see a body to lose your mind in. Look inside. I too have left you, to be yourself. I am with this rock, this sea, and with the part of you that is with me. The rest must go.

Understand. My silence

the image begins to disappear

he hears himself panting, feels his body moving, rhythmically, and his face under his own is disappearing, the body, disappearing...until, for a moment, he sees his own face, his eyes closed, his mouth parted in front of him he stands back, shaking his head, feeling round for his body. Feels a heaviness coming into him, his legs weak, has to sit down, out of breath

desolation

You must judge for yourself.

It is another voice.

You are what happens. Your spirit knows. All this is in you. It is what is, now.

I am speaking to you.

Open the jaws of the lion wide. Tell me the truth. Otherwise, you will die. You will die to yourself.

He crosses his arms in front of him, and leans forwards and backwards. Her angry eyes startle him. A compact of distilled memories he had himself forgotten begin to flood back with extraordinary clarity, as if it had all happened moments ago...

as she stands, in front of him
in her left hand an apple branch
and in her right hand, a brass bowl

Nemesis

he tries to defend himself, but cannot find words. He waves his hands about. His mouth gestures. A whole series of actions follow in quick succession. He is arguing. He is writing a letter, half covering it up with his arm, looking back over his shoulder. He is whispering down a telephone. He is smiling and talking confidently, holding court. The ringing telephone goes unanswered. He is pushing her hand slowly down the front of his trousers. His voice loudens as he shouts. You are trying to kill me. You resent me. You are jealous of me. She hurls a miniature rose bush at his head. He eases himself into her anus. I am not your bloody father. I am not guilty. I am...

and then it breaks. He is trying to kiss her. The door bangs. The engine revvs. He is alone.

He stands in front of her, looking into her eyes.

I don't know, I don't know, my intention was never to hurt.

What you do, you do to yourself.

So you must judge for yourself. I am here in the depths of feeling you have not understood. And I shall always be with you.

Love me. I am your death. You must speak me. You have no choice, but you will never love again unless you speak with my voice.

It is enough. I am in every woman's name.

Now let go.

The memory closes, and for a moment hands hold his face; he doesn't recognize her, dressed in white, dress and sandals, her hair pinned back, her face unseen full of compassion

fades into his own face, sunken and serious. And suddenly, he sees it. He grins at it. He sticks his tongue out at it. Old misery. Old deathmask. He tweaks at it with his fingers

and it begins to come loose. He stops, alarmed. It starts to come away. He scrambles to his feet, starts walking backwards; and falls. And then it comes away

sliding into his hands

his own face

he looks back at it

and begins to laugh

6

They drew him back to the centre, where he slept.

I was alone
And the ground was burning,
And I was' the ground that was burning
And the fire I was blinded in

But I dug
For dear life
Fast as I could
With a shovel,

Turning up the earth
As it cracked and burst

And flung me on my back as it fountained.

- awoke him
            floating
                       lying face down:

Coloured terraced steps of a ziggurat
reaching high above me
covered in plants and flowers...

Moonlight.

Distant voices, singing and whooping
carried across the water

'Come mad from the dark
Now silverlit hills,
Come and do not
Know how to enter

Come too full
Of my story to enter
Come too full
Of the moon of her to be seen'

And the moon
Risen, pink in the twilight
Whitening round and cool and full

Above the bay

Where the Goddess is rising
From under the ruins,
Where they splash in the water
With the temple, silent
Up on the hill behind them

                    .   .   .

Allright. Wake him.

He comes to, as fingers snap above his head.

Drink this. You'll be needing it. Her voice is light and playful. The fingers snap again, above his groin. He sits up. The women laugh softly.

He drinks. The wine is dark and strong, and the taste of it thick. It goes immediately to his head. He smiles. Two of the women come forward and start rubbing ointment over him, while another massages something into his hair. As he closes his eyes, the touch of her hands fills his brain with dizzy light. Then he notices her hands are streaked with green.

The Priestess looks down at him, benevolent for a moment.

Our Little Green Man. Come on, drink up. Is Kore ready?

Then we shall dance. Now (to him): stay close to the core of the dream, and you will enter. Remember. The core of the dream.

They begin slowly, at the edges of the circle, their hands linked together; their feet stamping out the rhythmn. Then they move in towards the centre, their hands break, and they raise them above their heads where the tips of their fingers meet, and they shout. Then they each move in singly, turning round the centre where he sits; they surround him, spinning round, rejoining the outside of the circle, till they are all alternately spinning and stamping their feet; as they chant:

This is the way we dance it
This is the way the spiral turns,
This is the cone of power
Thrown against the years

This is the dance of illusion
In a world without conclusion
This is the dance of clarity
This is our reality

This is the way we dance it
This is the way the spiral turns
And this is the way She moves it
This is the love that flows and burns

Moon-dancer, moon-dancer
Raise power raise power

Now!

as they stand together in the centre, over him, pushing their hands up
together. The energy floods up and down through him as he sits, his legs
crossed, his spine straight, breathing in deeply as the light builds up above
his head brightening and brightening

pyramid-shaped
at the height of one sitting
in a star of triangular gold

the walls of the Gallery
reaching above him

and the passage ascending

ends in two figures
Akhnaton and Nefertiti
robed in spectral light

Now!
Kore, dance!

She comes over, barefoot, in a thin white tunic, belted in gold. Beneath
it, she is naked. Her hair is cut short. On her forehead is a star.

She kisses each of the women in turn on the mouth where they stand back around the circle. His eyes still closed, the light hovers above the novice's head. Last, she embraces the Priestess.

The women begin clapping a beat out with their hands, together, and on the sides of their hips as they move, thrusting forwards.

The Priestess stands, her eyes fixed, as across the centre of the floor the snake slides towards her. She gathers it up, moving it round her body until it rises above her head round her arms and hands. Then she brings it back down around her neck, and above the sound of the women clapping she announces

> Tonight the moon is full,
> And Kore has the power.

She gestures to her, and then to the centre of the circle as his eyes open and look across to her. She looks straight back at him, and over him. Her eyes are shining.

Slowly, she traces the shape of the star between her eyes, and begins to turn. Her hands make sweeping movements out in front of her, and flutter. Pale yellow light begins to illuminate the edges of her body. He feels the ground beginning to lighten under his feet as he stands. She moves towards him, and then brushes past him, arching her back, and then round him where she moves her hands up behind him until they open out above his head. Then she dances round the rim of the circle, turning in front of each of the other women, as they nod to her. Then she returns to the centre, close up in front of him, and touches her finger lightly on the place between his eyes, and bringing her wrist back, opens it out slowly in front of his face. He watches, tranced, in silence.

Then she steps back, and moves over and outside the circle to either side of the Chamber, describing a long looping figure of eight. Her movements strengthen and become more staccato as her tunic seems to darken in his eyes as she tosses her head back and reaches out her hands, her palms splayed. Her body almost cuts the air as she moves, her mouth purses and hardens. Then she moves through the centre of the loop and her face lightens again, her body relaxes, soft and bird-like, white as the aura grows back around her, her mouth tracing the outline of a smile.

Then she moves back again, and darkens, her mouth open, her head back, drawing the side of her tunic apart, and stretching it round her breasts.

As she moves again towards him and smiles, she smooths a line down her body which moves out into her arms as they spread and she turns and arabesques, and returns to the loop where she spreads her legs flat on the floor and stretches her arms, one in front of her and the other behind her, as her head falls. As she rises, she motions with her hands untying a knot. When it is untied she gestures to each corner of the chamber with her hands, pointed. Then she draws him forward, and begins to move round him, the arc of her circling towards him

and the sound of drumming in his ears
alternating with the sound of water
where she darkens and lightens herself
between his eyes

flowing, as she softens and flexes; at one moment almost striding, and then swaying, rocking, the tunic beginning to cling to her, her breaths coming slowly faster and down through her, spinning, and then swooping round him again as she begins to blur in front of him, so fast and so agile

and she begins to dance in him
he feels it, his light meeting hers
at the meeting of light and light
noon and midnight, left and right

twin circles
                weaving
                        in her web -

as the beat changes and quickens
their hands clap faster
drum and river
drum and river
                as a shiver runs up into him

as she closens again

they mount the Step

the light streaming in front of them...

Come, you must dance now. Her eyes tell him. She touches his thighs with her hands. Her face gleams with sweat, the black round her eyes run down both her cheeks. He looks at her, and speaks, as she has spoken, with his eyes.

Lead me. I am yours. Take me.

She takes his hands, and places them on her breasts. His eyes mist over, he seems to be falling. But he is moving, dancing. They are dancing. The smell of incense thickens in the air around them, until all he can see is her; the walls of the Chamber have gone. His trance deepens. He feels her moving through him, step by step, effortlessly, running through his arms and legs and down through his chest between his legs. His stiffness melts away. And there is nothing left in his mind or his body, but her, only her.

I am yours. She laughs. Then her eyes catch his and hold them.

We must go deeper. We must linger.

He lies down on his back. Her mouth closes on his, her warm skin touches the length of him; and the sun-stone warm beneath him...and the smoke fading into light...soft white light, as she straddles him

Now. Become water. Flow.

And he does, the light enters him and streams through him...all sense of him gone into a point..brightening invisibly inside itself

as they walk forward together
white draped around him
a white palm wreath around his head

Come through. And he does

at last, merging with it...
throbbing in his ears...
and the white of it flashing
across his eyes he
moves
into
as
he
cries
out -

...and then, in the quietness, the stillness, she traces the shape of a star over her body

and he wakes, slowly, beneath her...

and she moves over the side of the stone and stands, drawing him up slowly with her hand; and smearing her hands across him from inside herself.

He stands beside her. They face forwards. She turns to him.

And speaks

Know that the hands
That have touched you
Are the hands of love.

And know that all between
My two hands belongs to Her.

She is here now.

And know this:
My love is you, but my love
Does not belong to you.
It belongs to no one but this.

So love me because you know me,
Love me if you know yourself.
I promise you nothing but yourself.

You are here now.
And as you have loved
So shall you be loved.

She draws him to her, and kisses him. The depth of it holds him, almost faint for a moment; and then she pulls away, holding his shoulders firmly as she does so.

It is done. Now, kneel. Place your forehead on the ground. Now, raise your head, and close your hands over your eyes. So. You are closed.

Now, come forward. Take the step. Be patient, you will return. You will return, now you have begun.

She smiles. It cannot come all at once.

Now go in peace.

She walks away.

He turns, but she has gone

the antechamber

Ahead, the door lies open.

the silence

he is alone

7

Desert become sea
                        become ocean,
And the sun
                become a white hole:

As I glimpsed this body's
                        floating forwards
high above the ground
                        dancing in the sky
the whole of me
                stretched freely
the whole of me
                beyond body and mind
                                  was sky, sky

-music, as I turned
with my arms my
head hung back

As the dead ground beneath
lay furrowed with white seeds

And the shadow of the temple
became a cross, a figure
with its arms braced,
and bent like a bow -

flung motionlessly from horizon to horizon

and on the sand below
the fragile etched glyph
of an enormous airborn bird

                    *

Came down
                and now, my steps turning back
the whole of it
                  silenced, brought to its ending:

Now I give myself back to him -
I pass the seed now -
I give my breath back to the wind -

I give him my eyes to make light with,
And I give him this body to labour with

Came down
                out of this Self, and was tested

between myself seeing
                        and what is

divided, as I stood

And I called to you, from a depth
in a voice suddenly overwhelmed by loneliness

Horizon I had to return from
unfinished self I had to turn back to

Long slow breaking down & breaking through -
and to embrace what is truly within you,
friend, you must enter this dense play of shadow
whose gift is a way of feeling, essential
to unfolding what is human

& it is easier to fragment than to make whole

it is easier to die than live up to your depth

to move safe and opinionated

than to experience the dilemma of becoming

what you alone are, a person

first singular on this chance of earth

chance to live, together, knowing

We are the creators
We the process

We are what happens

ta twam asi

each our own key
to the human mystery
in the air around us and from it
and found on the ground in front of our feet

it is no longer even a matter of belief

to grasp this simplest, and act, out of every day

* *

You came when all of this was gone
Behind me, abandoned as I was,
But the unsaid core of it continued
As I moved imperceptibly closer -
And into that crowded moment, waiting
To meet you: you on the edge of your
Body, dying - and how you came through
To say I want to live, I want to go on;
And how you took me with you, I cannot
Fully know, only the readiness, the strange
Clear ease with which it was given
This healing, prayer I stood for in your light
Following my hands somehow sure touch
Over where you were marked: *thank you*
Although I cannot see you or speak your name
Your face here in front of me,
In the shade behind the shutters at midday
Holding still afterwards together

And in that light I go back out in
And down the sea-track to greet you -
On the shore under the same
Unending sky where you sit, at one
With yourself

Swum out with you into the still
Level sea's splashing and laughing
And most of all, trusting, the way
You taught me

to lie down
                       & let it go -
on your back
                     in the water

and then calm...
                       facing up
                            above its depth

& then fluent as we lay
apart spread out, to sleep.

* * *

Corfu, London, Leros

244

in the year of light

'When that certitude came I felt as Dante might have felt after conceiving of Beatrice close at his side and in the Happy World, if, after believing it dream, half hoping that it may hereafter be a reality, that beloved face before his imagination grew suddenly intense, vivid and splendidly shining, and he knew beyond all doubt that her spirit was truly in that form, and had descended to dwell in it, and would be with him for evermore'

- AE (George Russell)

CLAIRVOYANCE

Snowfall lit up in the streaming early morning sunlight covering the roofs and the trees and the cars and the street -

waking behind the window misted over with ice, sitting, watching it clear as the snow begins to thaw, falling flakes my steps walked back to, to here watching an icicle hanging off the window sash dripping

each drop full of light my still half awake eyes stare into, the sky through each drop, and the sound of the light full of birdsong, and everything outside the window drawn into each drop, as it hangs, shivering, about to fall:

and in the quietness outside under the birds' high fantastic sound the soft pur of the milkfloat as it passes by in front of each careful slippery step a woman is making along the white pavement side as my eyes move back into this icicle, finger-of-crystal, mid-window

blending everything inside itself between my eyes as each drop becomes a bubble, and it steadies, slows, before it dots the sentence again with its falling...

I see you walking, naked, on dewy grass behind your face which fills this quivering light space in my mind as the thought of you hangs still; and it is as if I was looking through your eyes into your mind where I am seeing you walking, the ground stirring under your feet

and in seconds as the ground shifts back into a clearing among the trees where you have just made love, under where you both lay together, sprout five white snowdrops unfolding in the light as I turn the pages of a book in front of me that is full of pressed flowers and where your face was there is a basket full of dry flowers

and the flowers are falling onto the ground and the basket is dissolving and as each flower touches the ground it fills up with colour, now the air is full of scent and the air is warm and full of summer light I can hear bees buzzing very loud and very close nosing their way into the pollen, a light breeze...and the taste of the sea air in our mouths

and again you are walking towards me over the grass now your skin is tanned your fingernails painted red your hair full of long thick tresses and you are smiling as if about to speak and I understand your smile as you turn round and gesture back to where you have come from a year or so before, seconds ago, a drop ago

the big flakes of snow falling on my shoulders and on my hair as I open the front door and walk into the kitchen: and on the large spread yellow plastic tablecloth a small glass vase full of tiny daffodils lit up in a shaft of mid-winter sunlight...

trudging a trail of melting flecks of snow upstairs, and sitting here with you invisibly inside me suddenly seeing my own dead face mirrored in yours as your face becomes a blizzard of driving snow three feet deep round that dead house and you are trying to clear a path through it and you can't and I can't see for the tiredness in my eyes and the ache in my body and the numbness blinding me

and I am seeing a face in my mind I do not know whose face it is but it is light right at the edge of my mind where my death was going to for months that face until I found myself standing in a room full of people I didn't know and you were there turned slightly away to one side as I found myself beginning to walk over towards you in that split second as the room went silent and I could say nothing...the snow: outside now...the unmade bed behind me...the icicle's length tapering into its brilliant thaw-ing tip -

as you begin to turn round.

HEALING

And the house empty,
And there was nothing
But a few extraneous, scattered belongings.
We lifted them silently into your car.
Your face stayed set -
'We'll just do this and get out'
As you tried to smile...

Cold, damp air in and out -
The worn spread of wall-to-wall carpets,
The small blank windows, and the dumb walls
Where you thought *this is it and it's ending.*
I stood outside and listened
To the trees a hundred yards back being sawn down.
I stood back and listened -
At you then, screaming inside the house
And the searing of the live wood, crashing
And I waited for something I could connect to.

It's all packed up now, the boot door's closed
The key's under the stone and we're ready to go.
Johnny, the stray cat who was born here, mews
Unconvinced as you stroke him - and the moment
Reaches out towards its edge, and in your face
As I look at you glancing away quickly and down
As he rubs up against you with his cold lost eyes,
As you balance on your heels to stand, to say
There's just one thing left I've got to do.
I nodded, and hung back from you.

Then I saw the statue:
Slight, stooping, her arms drawn
Tightly across her on a small mossy pedestal.
And you, gone out of sight, as I began to walk over there
Reaching my hands slowly over the stone of her
Closing my eyes and going still and seeing your face
As I was about to see it, crying, your arms clenched
With the sick pain of it labouring in your stomach;
And I held my hands out gently as I was moved to
Asking, now, I'm here now, so tell me what to do

Give light, say nothing, just put her in light
As you came into my mind and so clearly
As your screaming became you whirling
Around and singing out beyond the house
In the knee deep grass in front of the larches,

And the sawing stopped as the image held
Your smile, your eyes in all their light fine fire
You as you are in that uniqueness that you are
Now you are about to leave all that your were here
Coming back, shaking, breaking down in tears
From where you stood behind the house and held onto it
Walking round once so as to let it all go
And take her hurt with you, to heal it
As she ran around holding onto the trees -
And as you move into the lightness of your dancing
Your voice I am vibrant with listening to -

Lifting my hands away and sending this to you
Giving it back to the light it was given to me through
As you start up the engine, and the trees begin to blur
Down the long track as the sawing starts up
And the abandoned girl's tiny frozen eyes
Gaze blindly, paralysed, down.

FULL MOON

I am awake now,
It is calm.

The crowded city night reels outside -
But it is light in here under this moonlit sky
And I know where to go to find the real darkness
Crossing this bridge and coming back to you
With the river moving in its fluid breadth inside me

Returning freed into your calm your light
Step by step holding onto nothing but this
Depth of feeling between us, reached beyond us
Its blessing suffusing us, gazed at
Through us, in its aura of
Clear-seeing eyes.

Alone in your house now the outside fades, the room
Flickers and the light on the walls gently vibrates -
You body is a candle flame, and the tips
Of the fingers of the flame touch lightly, waiting.
I sit and look into your eyes as we begin to change
As our talking peels away layer by layer
Into the dry sea of cars and shouting voices;
And we say no more words, moved to each other
Mouth to mouth, breathing the same
As it wakes and we watch it spread over our skin

Deepening as it brightens and the room closes in
Behind our eyes where we reach each other - kissed
Quickening into this limitless closeness, bonded
In the pull of this stillness within us
To be ready to be one with the wave
To come towards the crest of it
And let it take us -

Lingering in this linked touch of fingers and thighs
Merging, as you let my body and yours go, as it rises
Out of its blood-dark uncurling itself slowly into this
Heartbeat between us gone into its sway, shaking
Swept up and down the length of us: and holding it

As the room becomes a shell of light surrounding us,
As you crouch down covering me over with yourself
And then again, as you tip back your tilted face
Bathing in its quivering warmth you take from me
And give back from your breasts and falling hair,
Together, still, silenced, filled -

And no thought of ending, no thought at all
No past or future, nothing, until all there is, is you
My body moving with you within me, and your body
Arched back I am opened in you up at one with
Wholly as we follow each other to surrender
As you rise with your arms spread
Under the crown of your head,
Your eyes - closing - letting it pass, flowing
Down into the shape of us we have made on the floor -

Now there is light coming out of me and entering you
Coming down into me from you and you are light
And we are fire flowing up our backs and in our arms
And we are water falling beyond the edge together
The force of it curving up inside us and all over us
To flood each inch of our animal grace
This core our bodies so completely understand
Undone, shuddering closest of all, and unfought for
Finally - grasped, between our hands
Held stunned soundlessly - before the first words
Came back

As your eyes fill with tears, as you smile
And it is calm.

KNOWING

All of it at once, now - and wholly
Within it, without tension
Or division - and always and only
Through having let be, let go
To come here, come clear, to reach
The other side out of the mist of our mind's
Unmoving eye -

Come over the edge of the sea with me
Come back into being what the whole of your body
Can see: this sea in us, and the wind blowing over it
As we drive down, drawn, by its strong subtle magnet
That is the love that we are, sharing each other
Inside it -

Leaving the car by the high stone sea wall, walking
Out into its roaring rounding from offshore
As the tide of it arrives with us and fills us, opened
As each wave is flung against and up - over the concrete
Walkway; spumes of spray airy as our steps move
Down like hurrying to dance, come on, let's go -

And we do what we both know, you smile, in your element
And I let myself go wide, jump and spin round - the sheer
Energy of it as always wordlessly and all-welcoming, us
Into its rhythmn to translate it into *I love*, the
Inarticulate that only this body can speak, this
Unspeakable knowing that I am at last learning
How to speak -

Leaning out over the railing's edge, looking down into
This one wave's enormous curving trough, suspended, and as
It breaks shattering its foam-fall and is still, sucked
Back into its still always-about-to-fall shape -
As your eyes gone in swim in front of mine, and then closer
As your eyes become the sky's, your arms a part of mine
And the gulls glide riding the wind in your eyes
And my eyes move beneath yours and they are the sea -
And our breathing as we watch becomes the sea's moving,
I find myself swaying: and there is nothing

Left between me and it, you and it, you and I: this is it
And we are running back laughing, drenched, under the wave
As some kids in shiny soaked anoraks go as close as they dare,
And a large shaggy dog bundles and rolls where the next wave's
Crest collapses over him, all one and at once -

As a couple from behind stand uncertainly in the balance
Of where the next wave is already rising; both hanging
Onto a bright blue umbrella above their heads -

As we shelter up above with the window wound open;
Watching ourselves becoming part of its memory
Waken deep, as now, so that every time we see
That it is all one self-reflecting thing - we are moved,
Reaching out to it - invisibly - filtering inside us
To the quick light living centre of what we are:

when you & I & the wave are one
and we are the sea

NOTATION

Space: come out here into the sunlit morning park,
Where the old gnarled trees stand bare
Among people spread and scattered out
In this place's opening;
And in breathing the relief of it, begin
To clear the head of its haze of chatter
So that the heart can expand
As naturally as the sky does -

Walking, loosely, down to where the ponds are
Ripple-full of the fluid clutter of living sound;
Staccato voices in mid-sentence, cut in with dogs'
Panting and racing, past kids' shrill screaming
Shrieks, and coots' bleeping cries; ducks' flap
Of disturbed wings, and a single swan's skidding out
In a slow white flash on the water -
And in the water, letting the eyes
Loosen their fixed focus
And draw in the criss-cross eddyings
Of its trance:

Full,
To closing them, and to sit
Close-in to come into the stream
Of this continuous world unfolding -
That is each moment's note, and our note - the way
Everything notates itself and scores the moving air
According to its harmony, or lack of it -
And in as much as we can deepen to attune to it;
And bring the eye inside us out to see beyond seeing
Into being, as it is imaged inside each thing
As it words its wordless shape -

And we surround it, become music
With this silence, this space - that is

My body, your body's

Source of conscious self and wholly self-surpassing spirit.

THE WHITE POEM

'But that of which the observer is really speaking is altogether invisible, and he is perfectly aware that the light or colour picture which he gives has no more to do with what he actually perceives than, for instance, the writing in which a fact is communicated has to do with the fact itself'

- Rudolf Steiner

'You are spirits with a body, not bodies with a spirit - you always were and you always will be'

- Silver Birch

'All that is visible must grow beyond itself, extend into the realm of the invisible'

- *I Ching*
tr. Richard Wilhelm

Invisible world.

I have come to the edge of you.

Standing here, in my body, at ease, as if on air
Breathing in silence...

I have learnt to stand still.

Now the sea mist rising
                              a thin stream of cloud
Up the sheer
                   falling away
                                    dark stone cliff face
On the edge of where
                          the grass ends
                                             & the air begins.

I dreamt of walking along a line
I was naked in the dream
I was as I am

And to the left of my spine, my back
And one moving thigh calf and heel,
The half of him that was visible

Walking towards a sun
Along the length of a low broken boundary wall:

And then a little later on in inside time
I was awake sitting up on this jutting-out rock
I was cold and I was talking to you on tape,
I was opening as far as I could into the place

That is slow and which only the body knows -
This body of air
                     this space from which words

Occur and rise
                   to the mouth
                                    this sea of air

This body swims
                in its deepest speech into

This invisible space
                between the words
                                white space

Sky space
        sky page
                the real page

And it began as a disc of green oscillating light
I watched it come out between my eyes -
I watched it coming out of my mind - the low tide
Sand and distant twilight headland behind it,

As it became the horizon, and expanded
And was green and then yellow and then white
Light being given back, into me, from it

As it gently grew huge and whitened
And was a white hole a white sun and in the sun
A colossal figure was standing, the male
Or female body partly hooded in a loose cloak
And the face serenely in profile looking away to one side -
Irradiating light between my eyes,

And my eyes were open.

                .   .   .

I call this the edge of the world,
We are alone here
                surrounded here
                                as if on a mountain;

The path trailing off to the car park
And the cluster of hamlet houses
Their lead roofs and whitewashed walls -
The way you can look sometimes at something
Until it begins to disappear, its
Apparent solidity become light, the face

Of someone become featureless
                         presence
                                    become space

The foreground fading
                    the sea rocks
                                   blending in mist;

As you kneel and peer down to where a group of gulls
Hover round one of the rocks split by swirling froth
And past the tangled barbed wire fence
With its tufts of sheep's wool
                                 the cliff falling

Among scraps
              of abandoned material -

And out,
Over the edge
              watching a gull
                               flying out, apart

the grey mist white of it
                          beat by slow soundless beat

of its beak
            eye
                 and wings

becoming invisible.

                              2

Now enter this whiteness, where your steps are leading you
Back into that churchyard with its newly laid grave,
And the shock of suddenly all those bright twilit flowers
Taking your breath back -
                          and held it, bending down

Close where the rain
                      had smudged & blurred the handwriting

scrawled messages of farewell
to a dead man's soul
gone into the mist

gone into the mind, this human fleshed thing
become like a body of decaying words

gone out of the body into the mind,
as the thought the half-glimpsed image of it comes through

where we go through

from this charged place of him under the dug earth
on this edge where only the one sense can penetrate

to him that was him laid down here,
and him nowhere here at all, nothing at all

And as the waves roll in, coming in, out of the mist
Stirring in their white windblown crests

you come to the point
the point in my mind I reach
and ceaselessly fall back from

into the waves,
                    the waves,
                              the waves.

3

Something invisible in you brought you there
You came back, shaken, your tears blown away by the air
And told me. You turned from a trickling spring, saw it:
A great black cormorant splayed flat, its wings outstretched.
And then a gannet a few yards further on

And then a sheep with its belly ripped open
And then - your camera: jammed. And something unnameable
In you it took the whole week to start working through;
This intuitive fact of our being what happens
It is not fixed, nor is it random

But in that fluid space between, there, wherever you are
The place is you as strangely as you tell me your dream;
And that dead beach that haunted you was a mirror
Of all that it brought up in you, on the threshold

Of that dead life you died in.

4

Dead body of house behind rusting iron farm gate
Open to the wind and to everything

An empty bottle drinking in water from the stream
Reflecting the weeds like trees in the undertow

And the rafters piled among plaster, and broken
Slates; and past a fallen roof-section, the outhouses

Became blended totally with the brambles, ivy & nettles.
Stairs you could walk up into the sky on -

And the sky, the thin blue endless abyss of it
Curving from the top of my head where I'm standing

And then inside the open walls, four square spaces
Through the empty front door framing
Under the contact sheet magnifier

your hidden face
only you can enter
and in the shadow
                    of what the earth is turning & turning

through
            the shadow-whole of what you

have passed through -
                            intact

ghost of you
                    standing behind you

in your being that is living here,
this human ghost that is in shadow here

this valley of shadow you & I
are going through

this memory-landscape
                    dreamscape
                              dream of life

threading out, as we talk
inside and out

of its invisible
              lens-like
                        beyond sense centre

that is light,
the image exposed
in fluent light
              moving
                    behind each image

wind and wave sway
and mood of face
tone of voice
              coded, visibly, approximately

in process
of becoming the evolving
point of itself
              in the mind's eye
                              the source

at flashpoint
trigger point and each line
of this as we are together traced
                              along the length

of its opened-out labarynth
                        of outside & inside

and at their · of intersection
                        and across a threshold

that is blank white space
                    between us/each line of this

filling and then fading
                        each word of it you speak

on this air as it warms
                        in its invisible ink white

and then vanishes,
is revised, is replaced
- whited out, retyped -
                        begun again
                                    in the mind's eye

the body's source
                    at the deep interior
                                    the earth

meditates & your mind mediates -

on this side of physical life,
as the road bends round and the stout open fence
borders the white sun's sea

the bare sailless mast of a moored yacht
heavy length of anchor chain on harbour stone
and the body deliberately treading the ground
and a solitary white car accelerating out of the mist;

and my body lying
                    down on the pebbles, letting

the sea sound
                    cover me and the thought happen

thinking in white
                    textures of white...

fallen feathers
                    white sheets and the lines on this

cuttlefish, and this hand
                        and the blind touch

of a magnolia petal
                felt between finger-and-thumb

with the eyes closed,
walking, in step with each step
in my skin
          and the skin of you I touch

through the sound of running water, and behind you
as the firelight mounts
                                      in a time
                        turned inside out
        into space

5

World visible and invisible
Become thought, visibly -
And in my body, my body you can see
And in my voice, and that which speaks
This voice

as the print rises
              rubbed under your fingertips

up on the floating
             surface of the paper

And if you took away the space
From the atoms within me
I would become what I am behind this image
I would become that vanishing

shadow-on-the-gravel,
            focussed in this illusion

of spaced particles
          that shape him as human.

Midnight lunar aureole of light,
Crouching by the window breathing the night's cool depth
And over the surface of my skin

Beginning to feel

that closening
              tuned sense that these hands
                                    touch
around your head
               white figure, white presence

Distilled in skin, moonlit, bathing in it
Spoken in this clearness of your whispering voice
The sound of you in a being that is beyond ghost,
Come through in its full subtle strength

slow heartbeat tremor
                  the stillness vibrating
                              embodied

on the edge of each slow white second's ending

In a square of white developed space,
Edge where this visible world of what we are
Enters into its energy
                  the hand's slow moving
soundless sound
               of white on white, the traced letters illegibly
beyond me
          as it shapes & images each inch of this paraphrase

On the untouched pages
Of a book - a blank white book
Cover and each page I am turning - the whole thing

as I am standing in this
                 spirit body
                     Self that is here

From the body's depth, dreamt, drawn
Unfolding from its elemental image, earth -
Born bound and connected

to this air body of voice and speech
                        that is *I am*
                             sunk

in the shadow light where each life
                              is being written

And deep in the closening distance where you have come
To stand beyond yourself in this moment of your mind here

gone through the body into the mind
coming back to flood the body with light

This is the sacrifice
Crossing the threshold now beyond all holding back

surrendered
               filled
                         as with you -

And the whole of it brought back into this mirage
Of our dehumanized suffering nothingness
Plane of which we are the makers and the reflections
Death of what we are dying through
                                   into this whiteness

of spirit self
               filtering, worked
                         consciously & complex

From within what we are invisibly journeying towards
Beyond this shrunken horizon of ourselves,

from this co-
               nnection, source of our
                              extension continuing

as indelibly as we are continued -

Now it comes through as the sun fades to twilight

And outside, the silverlit leaf rustling wind

And in the silence where I have gone beyond him to meet you.

                                        Pembrokeshire & London

268

BEGINNING

Doing nothing about this,
Or the day, or the time.
I don't know and I don't know
Lying back with the light behind my eyes
Watching the mind stop -
Watching my watch stop,
Letting it all stop,
Letting it go.

Thought-free, as the light is
As I drop whatever words come, one by one
Into the light's depth, the lap lap of the water
And a half-buried book left open in the sand
With its torn bleached pages I saw myself
Slowly scattering into the water -
And pages and pages I just crossed out.
Standing in the water and the water was light
Splashing it over each other and laughing
As we talked to each other with our eyes -

And now you lie with your face in silence,
I look at myself dissolving as I step
Forward to where I can carry nothing
Only the light of what already is in me,
Becoming that self as it has always been
Endlessly begun, and about to begin.

coda

'The end only a beginning
of the gathering of friends
and a long light song
at the coming of night'

- William Arkle

ON FOUR PAINTINGS BY FRANCES MARSH

1

Here at the meeting of earth and sky,
Healed eyes' oneness seeing
Stream, hill and tree released
In the green liquid air

Showing us
That to think is to see,
See to feel
Earth as light
In the green heart's core

And so, in the foreground
Where your finger has touched
The long, rising stem of a grass reed

Parting its twin fronds.

2

Still life on the edge of light,
Glowing dimly through this transparency
The sunlight streams on under the framed glass:

Colour that is word and thing simultaneously
Flower vase, white jug and pale brown kitchen bowl

Out of this colour mist of air, earthed
Fusion of conception and fact
'Softness the hardest way' as Bill said,
Matter in the aura of its essence
Emerging slowly into focus
Over the table top:

Flower vase, white jug and pale brown kitchen bowl
Dreamt, awakened, made out of the body of what we are.

3

Christos in Christoph
Radiant and quiet
Bearded face and broad
Shoulders loose
His arms by his side,
And his eyes closed
Inward and awakened
His breath still
His lips sealed
The deep voice stilled
Peace of him shimmering
Around him, from inside him
Christoph as he is
Witnessed in your inner eye
Painted from the heart
You love him with
For himself, human
And with this vision
You have given him
To live for

Freeing us
Who have eyes to see
That we are in spirit now,
Each of us, living
What is living us, given
To us, to live, alone.

4

And this is your mystery -
Wait. Not a breath. Not a sound
And then again -

As the Grail rests
Contained in its shadow
Placed by the window
With the room behind it -

And, now, touching it

Light, from around the corner
Streaming towards it
Strange light, neither
Moon nor sun, but soft, white
Around its carefully smoothed
Protected shape

And not a breath
Not a sound

        as you sit

        invisibly

      about to stand up

      and walk, into it.

persona

Portrait by Carole Bruce

CHILDHOOD

A deep, braking bend in the road -
Coming back where I remember, where he once lived
For a moment, and with the sun full in our eyes -
And then the elm-lined avenue, empty - gone
The whole lot cut down; and then the house
Its whiteness covered over in a dull suburban beige
And the covering evergreen shadow it lay behind,
Exposed in blank cold light - the house
Remembering nothing and the outline of the garden
Snow-blurred; and only the dim twin waving tops
Of two huge Scots pines suddenly touched
The ghost I had begun to walk in, woken
Back to the surface - unattached, free to go
Back into my heart's imageless home

While the human half stays and remembers, we
Both talk childhood; and back a piece comes,
Back a piece of this life rushing and shrieking
Down through the sloping toboggan-snow -
And the sound of my father's car on the gravel
And the well at the front I'd climb down, none of it
That I could see there - clearer by far in me:
Strange, that. Half here, half not, and still knowing
Every step of the way up through the woods
Past where a nameless old tramp had shacked
Under branches and garbina bags, gone to earth;
Here, a moment ago in his mind, the half of him
I can say *I* to - and that part is ghost, is invisible
And I am walking in it - yes, of course, it is strange

Looking at you in this light, the warm blood flowing
Inside us between our held hands; and because you
Can see what's being felt, immediately, without words
I am wholly at home with you, sister, *I have known you*
And the whole thing here is recognition, seeing
That we are always being shown it - as fast
As a memory comes and goes, and subtly tunes us
A little closer still; as grist, as material
And is the meaning of living in a body at all -
This is the journey...over the still intact stile

Out where the grass is thawing under slats of ice
I tell you this is once where I first meditated
Where I first came out of that character I was,
Engrossed, half asleep, buried in me now, among
All the other reels of unedited footage

He flickers, illusion, seen through, seen out -
Till he is ready and it is no longer merely his own,
Remembering what he once was and is returning to...
The trudge up the last bit over the slush-sand
Up under the pines to where the church's shadow
Emanates sadness; and the man inside, the virger
Standing in a battered coat rubbing his red hands
With his loud broken voice and hoard of useless facts,
Imprisoned in the suffering parable of himself -
The human in him colourless, defeated, and full
Of unbearable longing in his homeless cold stone
Heart of a home: this church, graveyard where it
Neither begins nor ends: this threshold limbo
Of carved and lettered death - touched him, helplessly
On the arm, and bought a cheap plastic keyring
I slipped the key of my room on before leaving

And the sun between the trees burning in amber,
In the chill-towards-twilight air, realizing
We've got to get back now, moving a bit faster, can't
Stay here forever on this turning earth! - you laugh,
And if I never come back here I know it doesn't matter
And at the top of the last slope down, I begin to run
The sun already half gone under the horizon -

So one last time I remember the fields below, walking
Up through the dark to see the farmer's big rockets
Bursting up and falling, star-winged, out of the sky
And there was music in my head and I was happy
And the child is running down, jumping
Over the trees' long roots -
And with all of this I turn to you and kiss
Your pale alive ageless light face

This is how the song goes,
And here's how it ends:
Nothing visible remembers us.

SCULPTURE GARDEN

for Andrew Motion

A wilderness turned into a postcard:
Tinted green lawns and carefully overhanging trees,
Dredged ponds and renovated ideal home Tudor.
Up the bumpy mud track, a white horse grazing
Nibbles air into its stone mouth. I thumb through
Three glossy pages about how the place was made -
Into a pleasantry of saleable 'artful wildness'.
I speak from the wilderness.

Hang out, stand around, behave, stay cool: no thanks
I'll miss the speech and take a look at the stuff.
Passing his coked-out white face pinched with steel
And she, the hostess, with her sad proud accent, pointing
Out towards where each piece is positioned - and that
Failing sculptor-cum-lackey with his eyes full of mad
Helpless lust; and the Surrey air heavy and cloying
Thick under the threat of complete indifference
I said, I speak from the stone

As the day begins to deepen, into this green bowl
As the afternoon slides towards the falling light -
You could have easily sat through it all just thinking,
And then found everyone gone. Gone, their clothed bodies
Blurring, so light and insubstantial; the makers of this
Happy Hunting Ground, the undertakers, frozen in rictus
Smiles - caught in this illusion of being so-called human,
Dangled in the dreaming grip of the mind's eye
I speak of the mind

Walking behind its mask, papered over with words
Walking among bits of mind fixed in these textures
And our own minds, in the cut of each day, each line
Labouring under the weight of trying to be conscious
Makers of what we have not yet lived...and it drags,
The thought, held between the hands, and drops
Wants to lay down on the ground and let it all go
As these figures waft around over a void
My eyes gone speechless; and it surfaces

Anarchic, invisible and nameless

This goddess of the garden with her arms folded, breasts
Bare, her eyes looking away, not here; and this couple
Dancing together as they poise in that one moment
When you go right through your mind and become shapeless -
And the spread falling body of a woman surrendering, arms
Flung back and thighs in the swirling light through the trees
As I stand inside, and moving like her, am moved
As we have moved together and as I want to with you now
I would speak only of what matters

Of what is. And this carved eye tells me, with its pool
Of fallen rainwater and twig-leaves and bugs
Reflecting the dissolving shadow of our faces -
And this grave made in loving memory by a woman's hands
Placed under where all the white blossom will fall,
And down to what this garden will one day return to
The place that is the poem and is indestructible -
Turning back, now, towards the disintegrating party
Fucked over with its drum machine and posing troupe
Of adults murdering The Doors and Boy George
As the sun suddenly streams out over all of us
And over the grass and onto a maze, inlaid in brick
Circled round, and coiled, looped within itself
Drawing the whole garden back towards it
Into the creeping bird-filled shadows

I speak from the ending
In a voice that is voiceless
In a dream we are too frightened to understand.

AT BROCKWOOD PARK

in memory of
Jiddu Krishnamurti

The walls of the tent breathing,
Lifting through the sunlit trees outside
And the chairs packed on the damp mud grass
And your one hard chair, as always, sitting there
Stiller than breath, your hands reaching
Out in front of you: and your voice
Stilling each word, each pitched phrase
In the great realism of your old age

So let us speak together, without pressure
Or persuasion: let us speak as we are
Not romantically, not fantastically
Without the false ego of power
To be as we are, awake, here, and aware
Completely aware of every moving thought
And each slow sentence as you spoke
Moving us deep into listening
To ourselves, as you asked us quietly
How deeply can the brain be free of self-interest?
Can you simply remain quiet and watch?
Have you ever looked at people
Who have cried through centuries?
Can sorrow ever end?

And then coming back across the grass
Standing aside as everyone filed past
Come from miles away to hear you: and yet there
We all passed you, no one seemed to notice you
Invisibly at the centre of the day's circle
We crowded and chattered and ate food around
With you all around us, and as we could be
But so simply, having let so much go
To be that unadorned spirit you were
At the end of this long chaotic dream
Where all dreams end, and you are still alive
Standing on the same unrealized earth

Before you come to what matters: this unlived life
In a space tangled through with illusion -
And all of us, together, in it and continuing it
And yet to stand away with it all clear
Wordless and truthless and infinite - who
Can live as you have lived, and for so long?
And how, on this last and only edge of life left
The plain floor stage reaching behind you
Your eyes as if closed as you said the one word
That the whole of us, each of us, must become - death
Where nothing but this deathless essence is left
As the seed we planted deep in the valley of the brain
Blossoms the answer, and the joy of it
Echoing each syllable you said it with
Scored across the loneliness of your face:

And as I finally saw you, about to go in
Through a glass fronted door, vanishing
And not knowing if you would be waiting there
But walking, somehow in faith that you would be
As you were, and as you opened the door to let me in
Not assuming I had come to speak to you
As I turned, at last, with no words left
Nothing to say except thank you -
Your eyes and slight white-haired, light
Body almost shimmering - and then
As you nodded and grasped my hand
Because I could not speak, and you smiled
That unspeakable smile of understanding

That is, and is forever, goodbye.

in the dark

mens - moon
mensura - measure
menses - month

'Bright star, would I were stedfast as thou art'

- Keats

'The process of life consists not in unchecked progress but in the conflict between growth and decay. For this that we call the 'process of life' is not identical with the well-being of the form in which life is temporarily manifested. This 'process of life' belongs, not to a material world, but to a spiritual realm which underlies the material manifestation'

- Esther Harding

'The better the quality of the negative, the deeper the development'

- Ruth White

1. descent

NOTES

It is coming. The year is turning...spiralling, as the first leaf falls. I am told. To make ready. Where to? and yet I know. Some part of me already on his way. And I have been there before, yes. But this time deeper. This time. Again. Like never before

the higher up
the deeper down

- the fear of it. In my gut. This untrodden, only way on

& I don't know, only
that I must follow

•

Only echoes to guide me. A voice in the wind, whispering

Sound as of a great wind above my head,
And the echo of my footsteps rustling
Among the fallen leaves at twilight

And the sense of the body's weight returning towards the earth

The way he walked, slowly, in his battered tweed suit, with a tatty blanket half draped over his shoulder, and his long grey matted hair falling, his bearded face, his eyes glazed as if the street in front of him hardly existed

and the way no way no way the way
one by one we are being called down
into this darkness flowing beneath us

•

Black. Sheet of paper. Glossy black. Carbon paper. Illegible. Blank. Bottom-less. Out of reach of my eyes. Black. Blank. Dark. Echoes. Autumn. The sky beginning to close in. Faint mist of rain. Twittering twilight fall. Slow burn of bonfires. Bike skids in the mud. The sharp compass point of a church spire softened. The glow of windows in the water in ghostly streaks of fireside amber. Ducks, darting quickly in loose formations. Park wardens sweeping the leaves into raked piles. The smell of the rain like dust. The smell of the leaves burning like memory...and day after day sitting by the window watching them flame against brilliant wintry-blue eternal sky, and then fall, I can still see them, falling, turning, down leaving the bare branches of the trees' still dancer's skeletons

And the words their fading shapes on the page

And then the wind - cold - chill - sweeping gasps of air. And the body walking huddled, closed, inward. Ebbing closer

AND THE DOOR

It began in the light, I can see them now
Twin figures behind my eyes
Come down out of the house -

Sol with his broad smile and golden hair
Tanned, relaxed, standing there
And then Dark, down the stairs, braced
Thin, emaciated, head half-shaven and unsmiling

THROUGH THE WHITENESS

It began in the light. But now the light is dying

BACK INTO LIFE

moving out over the grass with the air rustling through the branches

IS THROUGH THE DEEP

beginning. A deep sustained note on the piano. Eyes shut, there is no score, listening   feeling   for the music   say it   as I hear it   see it   am, in it

DAZZLING DARK

DRAFT

Sound as of a great wind above my head,
And the echo of my footsteps, rustling
The dead leaves at twilight, a year ago
Now the year wheels round again to it:
I am being called down, there must be
Something I have forgotten

Your face first told me, standing there
The lightest face I have ever seen,
Entering this ambiguous shadow
That is the darkness of dying and not dying.
Your face, your red fingernails
Beckoning me into your white bed
'I will surround you with my water', you said
My friend, my priestess

I took the fruit you offered and ate
Smiling slowly back at you while we made love
As outside in the night, through the still
Warm air the dogs smelt us and barked.
And then, as I thought of you, walking in that dark
Up under the shadow of those high old trees
And out onto the grass, the low slight breeze

Its listening rustling inviting me to lie down,
Lie down as if I could roll over and sleep there
Pulling the air like a blanket around me
Safe there, and the mind thinking nothing
Be wrapped around behind my eyes
At rest, at last, freed from itself
With the feel of it - grass, tree-silhouette
And starlight, and the wind-note of the leaves
With each light gust up among the branches
Whispering *come, come* and then that dying into knowing -

But this other darkness that is dark, the other side
Of light lightless and helpless: it is the mind's
Throwing me into that long endless crashing skid,
And then in the body of that staring black mohican
That came down the stairs out of the house of myself

I could not control: this dark in our minds'
Depth that hungers for a grain of simple light
To surround it with when there is none -

And now your face again, this time in pain
Driven down as we walk as if on slippery stone
And your voice saying the ego must die, I know it
The theory of it, but nothing reaches its bottom
And the man who left the cave for the sunlight
Is called back; there was something he missed
Flickering deeper than the firelight

In the dark of what he could not name, and feared
Most, and was most of all - himself.

DREAM

Shadow woman, glorying in your misuse of power
Under the masquerade of your femininity,
What do you want from me?
I don't want your darkness
And your killing eyes
I know your vengeance
And it is loveless
I know your power, and it rules
Over a wasteland -
I know your desire
And it is ice

Wide open, all around me, but flat, and featureless, no trees or hills, no-
thing growing. I am sitting outside a pitched tent, and it is dark. I can
see him sitting there, trying to think...*I must have come out here, but I don't*
*remember leaving, I don't remember...it's confusing...*I have the feeling only that
I am being dreamt. A slight quiver runs down my back. I open my mouth
to speak. A man is standing in front of me.' You can see her', he says
to me, 'I know where she is'. His voice, sounding enthusiastic, his face
fading quickly in front of me, his presence calculated to last exactly as long
as his message took. So what is he trying to tell me? but already, I am
on my way, my dream body thoughtless, being magnetized back towards
you, and my heart full of old hope. But it's a false alarm. You haven't
changed at all. We are sitting, awkwardly, apart on a large sofa in front
of the large dusty windows. A cold white light fills the room. Neither of
us can speak. Neither of us moves. We both wait. There is dust everywhere.
We are both dead. Neither of us have been back here since we died. I can
feel my energy steadily being taken out of me. I can't even look at your
face. The light is making my head feel dizzy. I can taste the dust in my
mouth. I am trying to stand up. Somehow, I am dragging myself out

Again: I am standing beside you, but in a flash I realize that this time it's
different, I look for my protection, my distance, but I have none, I look
for my anger but it's gone. All this as my eyes glance at your face, and
you are smiling, and I watch myself like a puppet making those conciliatory
gestures designed to please you and not upset you, feeding you with con-
fidence and self-esteem; and so I say the flat looks fine, it really does, and
I can feel you closening as I talk, becoming increasingly uneasier, my
unfinished sentence hanging in the air in front of me as I find myself follow-
ing you up the steps and through the white door inside. Again, the room,

as it was, unchanged as I stand looking at the dim gold-coloured sofa still covered with its fine layer of unbroken dust. But your body has changed, even from a moment ago, and these tight pink curved silken trousers you are wearing, you've lost a lot of weight, you seem taller, and your face - is changing, it is tanned, deeply, and it is older, and I can feel its power - wait a minute, *who are you*? your eyes meet mine and I can't break their hold. Hecate. I try to move but I can't. Your eyes begin to fill me as you stand there, your clothes slipping away from you without your appearing to move at all, and then as you reach for me, touching me, it is still as if you have not moved, and I am standing there, and your eyes are fixed on mine, as my body almost faints onto yours, and I am breathless, my mouth over you, your back arched, your skin almost black in the half-light, and then inside you, as your face flickers between your own, and hers as I suddenly realize *I am betraying you*, but it's too late, I can't stop, my eyes are closing, I am turning, round and round headfirst diving down her breath loud in my ears my heart drumming the smell of her oiled skin the taste of it hungrily clouding my brain

By the sea now. The façade of a lavish, crumbling building, partly obscured by thin white swirling mist, and immediately, I recognize it, I know I've been there before, he knows, the dreamer, I can feel it stirring in him, a cold sharp shiver in his face which for a moment is not my face at all. Then we are waiting outside the door, about to be ushered in. The place is a hotel these days. As soon as we step inside, the feeling returns. The coldness. The manager stands in front of us, smiling. The clientele move around behind him from room to room, in full evening dress. The building is slowly falling apart. The sea is rotting its foundations. The manager explains, as he politely tries to persuade us to donate money for its repair. We are standing in a room that is covered from floor to ceiling in expensive shiny green satin. The waves are pounding outside the window. The building shakes. The spray flecks the glass. The manager continues, apparently unnoticing, suggesting that we buy over the entire premises, his smile hovering icily around his lips. Suddenly I am alone, walking down a steep flight of stairs. You have disappeared. So has the manager. For moments as the waves rise to break, I can hear voices and drunken laughter. The party is in full swing. My feet retrace their steps. There is no way out. We are trapped. And the building is about to fall down

Calm daylight fills the room. It's over. You are making the bed as I speak, telling you how the effect of what came between us took away my time and took away my self. I talk quietly as I move about the room. I am simply trying to tell you the truth as I saw it, so as to clear the air between us. You listen as you draw the sheets up, pausing, and nodding, and for your part, apologizing. All we can do for now is accept what has been and leave it, as it is, without revision. I just want us to stop preying on each other's minds. I shan't say much more, I've no wish to hurt you, you've told me your truth and now I am telling you mine. And then I'll go. You once asked me what you thought our last conversation would be. This is it. Then, the next moment, as I turn to the door, it opens - and you - *you* walk in. I move quickly over to protect you. What are you doing here? I don't understand, wait a minute...then we are both sitting on the edge of her bed. I put my arm around you. She sits, apart, at the corner. She begins to speak, looking down past her hands onto the floor. Her voice is quiet. She is complimenting you, and trying to make you feel welcome. She is being as nice as she possibly can. She is standing, turning to you, lightly, about to go out of the room to make coffee for us. Then, I can't think how, but I am standing back by the door just as I was when it opened, and I turn round, looking at you, sitting on the bed, and she is sitting beside you, her dark hair beside yours, light, in a shaft of sunlight as your heads touch and your hands close slowly together

---

'The worst comes last. What little control I had has now gone'
'If you could just let yourself fall'

- nightmare, you again, shadow of us together it's not over its hardly begun, no choice, the darkness is being poured over me, sticky and black, from head to foot, there's nothing I can do, but hold on, hold still, barely even that -

You draw me into a public lavatory and bolt the door. The place is full of bits of screwed up pink tissue paper and shit. I lean against the door. You move about quickly turning all the basin taps on full so that no one will hear us. Then you bend over one of the basins with your hands grasping it on either side, your pants dragged down, your pale buttocks facing me as I fuck you, the taps streaming, the room filling gradually with steam, the sweat running down your back, my thighs bumping up and back, and there are flies in your hair, and crawling over my back, prickling like tiny needles, as I catch my breath, panting, the blood taste of it in my mouth as I catch you looking at your face in the mirror, your mouth parted, your eyes glassy, as it mists over and the sound of the water loudens, running across the floor, my feet covered in wet tissue and shit, as the flies reach my face, I screw my eyes shut, I am beginning to weep, your voice rasping *hurry, hurry* as it begins to rise from my stomach, I can feel its column of air rising as I open my mouth to let it out, shouting this one long sound

293

going on and on as I fall

Then he is standing in front of me. It is him, again. Half-dressed, I can barely stand, still can't see his face. I hear him repeating the date when we will meet, as he presses a key firmly into my outstretched palm and then disappears into the darkness in front of me, and all around me, as I realize I am alone. I look down at the key in my hand

it is yours

JOURNEY

And you are my light
At the end of the darkness
My darkness, my light.

Far memory...in snatches...out of sequence. I am back on the mountain.
I have come back from the edge of light. I am retracing his steps, drawing
him back through the faint glittering skein of the years - only to find that
it is still unfinished, that there is no one summary trip: only the pattern
changes as you twist the mirrored tube...seer and seen where there is no
seperation...linea negra of light and dark...and this time, the ground has
deepened; and this time I see him as he was for real, I see how the light
reveals the shadow, and needs to...crossing old bands of emanation, their
intensity as fresh as ever...in the memory, where nothing dies...in every
body he has been...and this time, no face to hide behind and this time,
body, you are your own guide - no voice to talk about it, to talk your way
out of it:

I have been
A child looking down a gun barrel
An adolescent lusting for every passing cunt
A man unmoved by other people's suffering
A mind that has lashed out with a flickknife full of words
A body that has been a mere object among objects
A soul armoured with the power of heartless control -

and you
and yes
& all of us
turning on the spiral
on the wheel
turning
& returning

into this declivity
of dark wind and slush ice
now the moon is dying
hidden
behind the passing cloud

where the light at its height

begins to fall to this peak of depth
death in life and life in death
this is the threshold
come out of the mind
come out of my eyes
all around me

I see him half-hooded in a long black cloak, I see his skull covering itself
over with my face: tall forehead and hawk's nose...his steps echoing...his
face sketched like a pinned up photofit, spiky hair and leather jacket

where the seam of the valley of shadow runs on
where the autumn leaves spiral, blown towards the tunnel's mouth -

the lights of another town passing outside
moving above the rhythmic blur of the railtrack
a clockface lit up like a disembodied head
our faces' silent ghosts reflected in the window glass

And as you talked, your head aching and your speech confused, as I
glanced out of the window across the midnight street

As a child's face comes into my mind
The face of a soul that has just arrived
With the burden of its wordless memory
That we carry, unconsciously
In the shape of each body's
Written-out gravity

(turning the rough pencilled handwriting in front of me)

And that self diving to be born
Leaving its serene all-feeling form
And those eyes in memory
And yours as they gaze at me
Full of their knowing
That we are hidden, at a depth
It takes lifetimes to reach

what all of us are here
in the darkness, alive
living in time

timelessly
each
specific
life

in the mystery

Crossing the broken ground
Through each shed skin of being
Through all that we have been
In this one humanity

'in which the full range of experience has had to be yours'
as she spoke, with her angel standing behind her
the autumn sunlight filling the windows
her black & red gown with its broad raised sleeves
shining on the star hung round her neck

ancient - wisdom - misuse - expiation

and so the light must darken to be reborn
the light at times must go out of sight
blank page black page

deeper than our eyes

& our pain as always that we are unfinished
& the length we must travel beyond the mind

into the heart's
dark where the sun
is a black circle
burning: enter

this journey down in the other direction

unknown - uncharted - ½ of circle

(in a small & ever darkening space that seems to lead nowhere)

groping to understand
at the point where the mind stops

no voice...no guide...dark landscape...starless night

walking in the winter light
blazing across the water,
the wings of the ducks
silhouetted black as they fly
the path between the ponds
covered in dry leaves
and where they lie
under the water's edge
so clear and intact

reflected image of a woman sketching
her bent head and open pad
mirrored in the still depth

standing, leaning over the bridge
with the train gone behind me
and the moon's full reflection

below, deep in the water
a thousand feet down
webbed among the branches

the sound of the stream-flow further up
dark river coming to stillness here

the moon glowing pearl-white
the dark air freezing around me

your voice saying 'listen to the earth'
the room that night vibrating with presence
and in that light, on the other side
I saw around his head
& coming through his face
composed, in hair ears eyes
lips jaw and nose

flickering, and then gone
echoing, and then gone
ahead of both of us

wagging finger and sullen face
unreachable under your old peaked cap
and then as your pride dissolved in tears
and into one language in the sunny wood
and after so long now on the loneliest road
where and when and how to head for home

further and further north into the land of ice
the snow flaking past the moving window
the visibility almost nil

the whole thing
frame by frame
coded in a dream

scorpion I held at arms length with a stick
and as you sit in your fine, fragile humility
telling me how you'd found your child
alone out there on a small sheer stretch of cliff
classifying thousands of tiny wild flowers

as the daylight hangs
white above the mill stacks
and now the dawn halting
smoky from the hotel window

a spire's
tip
poised
in the
speechless
air

your hand
waving, your
smile
filling
the coach
window

terminus, facing this slow descent
the loop stretching   back   and round
sitting back, eyes closed, blank to the video
and now the zappy snappy fabby record DJ patter

follow the signs...the snatches
of talk...each flickering image

'the moving finger writes, and having writ, moves on'

coming slowly up into consciousness
to waken, blinking awake in the dark

-ness groaning into birth all around us

the night train shunting nuclear waste

the tunnel secreting its river of newsprint

in the mind deadened by a huge spreading ganglia

the scales tilting towards the harvest

the dark peak shining under the black sky

        & can only
        climb it
        inside this
        shadow

        & fall to it
        letting go
        into the unknown

        world without
        end within us

as the flame sinks lower and lower
to a point of light as the city closens
hovering clear eyed and detached

        to follow
        the felt
        encircling

                    thread
                    through

    'before the dream slips out of my reach
        before it goes back underground'

                as the window lights
                in the water
                go off, one by one
                leaving the surface
                empty and silent

                & then as we stood
                watching the hill's brow
                etched against the orange glow,
                framing an empty bench
                facing the skyline

    as our eyes moved past a clump of bushes
        to where a blurred form waited

                to come to life, turning
                a figure, out of stillness
                began walking, slowly
                down the path, surrounded
                by shadow, glowing, tall

                slowly shrinking

                in between
                my eyes.

IN THE MIND

Now I blink awake in the dark   . eyes and no face in front of me   sitting, leaning, forwards on a stone   . talking to you   talking   staring at a spot on the floor   where the floor was   now blackness only   and the sound of your voice as if singing a ringing note   fading at the edge of my ears   and something that is me   sitting here but I can't see him

speak him   hear him   think this image it   all of it   sunk   stuck   .   I speak, I mimic the actions of one who is visibly here   but when I close my eyes   even for a moment   this: blank black page

I cannot read   write on   the hand's movement across it   suspended on air   leaving no mark   words   no sooner written down   words   than they disintegrate   senselessly   repeating them   their sound become incomprehensible

and I think speak I must   the only way to surround this   abyss   and the head hung heavy becoming its vast black emptiness   and I think *I must speak or die*   and the body, unmoving, gripped with fear   that part of you here   on this unlivable   illimitable   edge of life waiting   always sitting, apart   waiting   alone

and I roll   roll   roll like a stone   down to the dry bottom   lying there gradually   blinking awake   must go into it, now   must enter it:

river   standing there   touching foot's tip   and then wade into it   and then, for a moment, swim   .   dark water like air come out of him he enters   asking   is this danger   no answer   only stillness   the water pitch black   soundless   .   cold   freezing   but feels nothing no place no journey   nowhere

across this, to the bottom of this   no answer . this is the world of the
unformed, the unborn .   out of this comes everything we are   down
diving down   and then rising   in bubbles of light   the water glowing
around him   towards the sunlight

and then turning   down again   the moon huge   gliding behind black
scudding clouds   as a drop of water sends its whole surface rippling
arms stretched in front of him   and the body dark   flickering, between
his eyes   spreading its darkness behind them   from earth to sky in the
mind

and then float   walking   weightless   white ground   the water become
sky above his head   and then, river again, on its borderline bank   and
cannot see beyond it

what was God's face   become a womb   now the darkness deepens   as
he shrinks rapidly   back through the years   his body, reversed   become
a child   become foetal   become the water   filling his eyes   surrounding
him   through the pores of his skin   entering his blood   bones   fish-
belly all around him   as he floats to turn   dim, blurred   struggling for-
wards   out of its mouth, this mouth   the first breath, cry, word

as if gulping air   quivering from head to foot   and how to swim back
that far back   to come back through   holding this thread

and the moon shining   fully in front of him   standing, feet apart, framed
in its light   streaming through this silhouetted shadow   turning to you
as the water becomes your body   merging between us endlessly

understanding, unforced   sinks back, exhausted   flat out, on the
floor   the weight pushing him down   slowed   ground down, to the

ground   /   each still-born step ˚ /   out over the moorland   /   scoured
by the icy wind watering his eyes

and by the daylight river

its being as if apart from him

its fluid release

unable to enter him   /   standing on the bridge   /   watching its
edged reflection   /   glow like black flame

and the road stretching back ahead/driving with lashing rain/peering over
the wheel/down a tunnel of bobbing headlights

into the mind's black/blank to passing faces, numb/sitting in a backyard
listening to the drains dripping/the rain falling, the soaked/concrete sur-
face slimed with green/the dead shapes of leaves splayed/& curled

huddled, sunk, shrunken aura
each flake of snow falls
soundlessly through

vanishing into nothing

stuck, staring

stops
dead.

2. level

SENSES

Darkness light, reached behind eyes
Behind words where the body becomes an eye
Groping for a way in to wake there
I had to become as if dead
I had to leave my eyes
I had to leave my mind behind

Feeling across this keyboard, fingers spread
To sense each syllable of its unwritten sound
As it echoes around me, with the score sheet empty
And the music telling me if I can listen
To its rippling glissando as it slows down low
To a single note that almost dies away, until
It begins to build back, rising from chord to chord
Now I am letting this darkness fill me
This piano play me

And the choir in black, massed before the altar
The cold stone air lifting with their voices
Up above the organ, sweeping up like wind
Wind of voice light floating in a sea of voice
Above the dancing conductor and the dead Latin
The words sung as breath from fifty breasts and chests
Shining from their throats and the O of the soprano's
Open mouth, coming up around their heads
Sung into this altered atmosphere

Lightening behind my eyes through my ears;
Surfacing, only to be called down still deeper
Humbled to the face of the living earth, sunk
Become a cthlonic space in the dark, to reach
This mountain's reflection in reverse
I had to become nothing
I had to lose my name
I had to die to the light to bring it
Back into my body

The gesture you made with your hands
Smoothing down towards the pit of your stomach
Your steps echoing underground where the stream
Flows past the cave floor under your bed
Where we looked each other's animal in the eye
Our stomachs turning together like tongues
With the fruit's blood staining our skins
With the seed we passed from lips to lips
And the rosewater tanned black tang of you -
My heart a blood soaked sodden rose
Waking as soft as grass covered in dew

In each sense made fresh, made new: so stop,
Still half asleep, to smell this flower
Its sun petals and flaring orange trumpet
Its stamen scent invisibly sweetening my mouth
And the back of my head bathed in winter sunlight
And the back of my brain bathed in spring light
Silent as a buzzing begins to hum in my ears
As out of the front of my forehead a bee crawls
Poised, sucking at the nectar, fluffed, the sense
Of it all over me, this body, woven into everything

Stirs in its chrysalis of consciousness returning
Standing as the skein parts, holding earth and sky
Level on the snow-ground with these stones around us,
Our hands held, breathing it up through our feet
Into the stillness a jackdaw's cry flies fading through -
Where the birch trees' flaming branches
Touch the sky of our slowly parting smiles.

ENDING

Dead body in black water.
The same place - stream, river, ocean
Under a sunless and moonless sky
And finally could see no way ahead
And lay in bed in the dark, fighting
For the last spark of flame
Behind tear-rimmed eyes.
Give me back my light
I want to be born,
Do you hear me?
No answer

Only the soundless, impenetrable water.
And your voice around me, guiding me in
As I stumbled in my mind between fragments,
Straining to glimpse my body wading in to swim
Saying this time I'm going to reach the bottom
And not caring if my lungs burst on the way
I was going to get to the end of this -
And can I lay myself down totally in faith
Without still clinging onto this mask of mind?
Can I be faceless and thoughtless and hopeless,
Can I be *nothing*?

It's hard to be nothing, and with no pride.
So I wade back into the water and swim out
And I'm still thinking I've got to go down
And the image is still blurred and hazy in front of me,
Bitty and distracted - and you with all your patience
Waiting for me to fall silent and begin this ending
So it's over, finished, he was going to dive down
And bring up I don't know what, maybe some black pearl
But he's lying there, face down with his bones showing
There's nothing I can do for him

So I go in to get him out, leaning to shoulder him
But as I turn back, he has changed - he is tiny
He is a child with his head lying tired and sleepy
And my body has become an old man, standing on the bank
Facing the dark stretch of land in front of them

307

Now they are walking, the old man with his staff
And the child on his back, and then beside him
Holding his hand, surrounded in a blaze of soft light
And both of them so clearly, now the old man is sitting
His bearded face and brown eyes scanning ahead
As I ebb back slowly, leaving them there
As you close the door on my lying here quietly
Fingering this gold medallion you have leant me
As the old man shoulders the child out of the water
And it is him, him and the boy

And his name is St. Christopher.

SELF AND SOUL

Soft light silence under the sky's blue
Emptiness of a long beach, sloping brown cliffs
Deep inside where you wake, huddled, tight
To slowly begin to stretch, to take
Your hands away from your ears -
Shell-wind blowing through them, shut eyes
Opening, blink to the light, and the wind
Silenced, and the place intact

As she glides by the water's edge
Horns and tail and whorl of shell moving
And where your fingers loosened their cliff
Their mountain grip: where your being could strain
Its winged spread standing no further -
You fell to this, you listened
Your heard your own voice saying
'I can't keep this up any longer'
As the first wave of sleep rolled over you.
I speak of what has gone unconscious
I have come here, knowing only this unknowing

So I ask her how she feels, and the watery
Sand ground slowly soaks under the length of me
And how does she live here, and under her grey face
Tiny teeth feed at the wave's sipping edge
And I ask her how she feels me, and my back
Rises into this shell-skin covering
Now I begin to answer you from inside it
As a quivering spreads from my head into my feet,
And I tell you that I have become snail flesh
Soul-flesh, no longer self, but soul
That is small and which speaks very slowly
Leaving this weaving of its glistening trail

Snail feed on plants at night in the garden
Snail hide under this damp log by day,
And snail need rock fluid to build its shell
To inch each step along this slippery way
As the feeling began to reach the side of my head
The balance beginning to falter, the mouth to stammer

And around the unprotected flesh there is danger
Now you must curl back into your safe place,
House with its doors and windows closed
Body with this glimmering guiding each action
Simply and practically and with due attention
Calm and contained and at one with the ground

Waiting for our light's sap strength to return.

3. emerging

CLEANSING

Now take this body
And let it be still -
Let it stir from within
Slowly as the feeling
Unfolds and surrounds you
The close touch around the head
The voice sunk in the throat
Laid out, laid flat, arms and legs
Draining their urge to move
No longer conscious of themselves
The mind, no longer fraught
Wrestling, fighting for itself
But still, become a point
That opens as you step
Out between your eyes:

To field, lake, waterfall and glade
For five days this ritual of cleansing
Walking to the lake's edge and undressing
Taking these worn out creased black clothes off
And leaving them to go into swim, to slowly
Quieten this struggling over the strained
Surface of the water, stroke by stroke
Until you reach round to a waterfall
Wading out to stand under it washing
Your face and chest and thighs all at once
In its streaming down over you
Naked as you go through a gap in the cliff
Walking in the light soft clear air
Along a path towards a glade
Full of warm dappled shadows
Where your new clothes are waiting,
Hung over a branch

White dungarees, and then a white habit
In which I went aside to pray in silence
And on the third day the lake was golden
The water like an ointment flaked with colour,

As I swum in its deep calm under, and up, and under
Standing at the waterfall's threshold pouring
Down over my eyes from the crown of my head
On the other side where the mind is healed
Where the mind becomes your unclothed being
Body in its simplicity treading the path
To put on this glittering weightless suit of gold

And then on the fourth day's night the darkness
The lake's surface rippling with moonlight
The sky empty to the furthest star
The water warm and enfolding, the swimmer's skin
Blackened and dripping where the lake bore him
His body moving at one with the darkness
Of the water he stepped from onto the ground
His body shining black under the moonlit cascade
His eyes with their star strength inside him
And his white clothes loosely and barefoot covering him,

Then the last day: the field thick with ripe corn
The lake's edge alive with birdsong
Crossing back to it under the rustling trees
The stalks of wheat, the mud-ground and his feet
As clear inside him as outside - the lake bottom
With its flowing weeds, and the blue sky's clouds
Moving as he floats in the mirror of the water
And the waterfall's plunging white spattering foam
Bracing himself under its coldness wakening him
Into a dream that detail by detail is real
His eyes' blurred vision sharpened
His senses spreading back all around him
Lingering on the sandy path to pick up a stone
Turning it over and over in his palm
And not the word stone nor the thought stone
But this, and this nameless butterfly
With its blue-black patterning spread across its wings,
Quivering, about to fly

And this dream body become your own
In the glade where you slowly put back on your clothes
And in the tread of your feet on the stairs
Out towards the street -

and in the silence
before you begin to speak

SOPHIA

To know, the way you know without knowing how
In the depth of your body where I would follow
This child's pointing finger to sense it, the way
A bird flies gliding to swoop down, and then round
Drawing these colours across the page -
To have the whole mind guided
Threaded through its own effacement
That opens it back out to the world
That simple dead world it thought it knew

You have taught me to dream, the way you do
By drinking the dream in with its strange blood
That we discover is our own: there is nothing
Apart from us, but ourselves: so I surrender
To listening and seeing every day now, watching
Each day's teaching unfolding, as you told me
About the horse you'd dreamt of filling the stable,
And you with its power, yours, to own

As he came to take you to yourself, standing up
Entering you, and crossing himself across you
To tell you that now, take care, you are pregnant
And then at last as you lay on the floor
And your breath offered you the drink and you took it,
As I am taking this - labouring, as you spoke of it
A moment before it came to you - your birth
Begun in your mouth letting the sounds come
Numb in the hands, and arms, head, turning
Into your stomach

To come out, spread, from your legs
As your tear-filled smiling, laughing self.

LACUNA

Waiting. Frozen. Stillness.
The winter ground, the tread of our feet
Over the iced slicks and the dead leaves,
The grass bleached dry savannah brown by the snow -
Waiting, waiting: the lake frozen over
And a hundred birds packed in a single thawed channel,
And the deer sitting close together under a tree
And the gravestones leaning hunched, over a wall
And the great orange lunar sun hung, setting
In the frozen immobile air

Come out past the edge of darkness
Where the water has frozen white in the daylight
Come out, to tramp my feet back to the ground
And walk in unbroken silence, letting the mind's ache
Sing up in the black branches, behind the numb mouth
And clenched, pocketted fingers - standing, waiting
Three hundred yards out there on the ice -
Going with the earth that knows what its doing
When the ice will split and heave
And the seeds rise in their first fragile

White flowering light -
But what of the mind, on its legs and talking head?
What of this world's weight of undrained poison
Pressing down, and us full of it, dragging its dead shadow
Sunk like dreamers in a dreamless sleep -
Hardened, to the kill, without the time or faith
To suffer the naked source of our life-depth
Pushing onto the nine o'clock train, roaring
Round and down towards the runway overhead
Screeching its blinding blue echo
Into the wound of each defeated brain
And what can stop us now, but this standing here
To find ourselves, fearlessly
Flame-like and still
To take this dying world
Inside us, until
Its cry stirs now
To come through and begins

To open out, into a million-limbed flower
Of skin and teeth and hair and clear seeing eyes
Spread across the earth, under one sky -
Until the spring's steel fist
Crumples back into dissolving ash

And we learn, at last, how to live.

at Le Plan

for Ruth & Gildas

'True knowledge is intelligent love'

- Alice Bailey

'No matter how much you learn within your present finite knowledge, it will never be even one step closer to an understanding of God, the universe, or yourself. Knowledge, as you presently understand it, will never bring you closer to Life'

- Raphael

THE FOUNTAIN

Born

to the light's return

born

to this first day's

dawn

valley stretching beneath

mist above the thin borderline of road

distanced drone of cars

beneath the grey cliff-like wooded hills

below the wide tilled curve of vines

their gnarled twisted up-
turned roots, wrought
proof, and in each tender
green beginning shoot

the earth
opening
under this
immense

cloudless

clarity of air

The house still quiet
sleeping towards the last hour
of its dream thread

webbed

where the centre opens
& you wake to a climbing tractor
to walk out through to where the sun is

rising

Clear mortal
shape of your body
stepping down beside this channel of water

the almond blossom's lit whiteness
scenting the charred deadness of
that winter tree

you have been cut down from -
hung, upside down
the grave clothes dissolving

your dream body

waking

naked and light

skin covered

in cool dew

the earth breathing
its slow breath under you

Standing by the fountain, to meditate
the sun's clear silence
filling your eyes

and your throat, heart
and down

to the soles of your feet
each pore of skin drinking
the earth
and sky's
blueness in

till there is nothing left of what
was you but this

fountain

rising above you as you sit now

its fed jet
hissing up
& in you

the bright
beads of water
falling

dancing
on the surface
where your mind was

bubbling
and then floating
like tiny stars

sinking
each secondless
second suspended -

drawn back to their base
thrusting their unbroken chain
of transparent blood pumping up

through you -

invisibly

with your arms resting
on your crossed legs, the finger
and thumb of each hand joined and poised

the silver
beads of water
inside your eyes

leaping up
in the blue
towards the sun's

eye -

shining through the particled length of you

and beneath
your body
become water
revolving and rippling
round between your legs
in its rooted encircling
stone-cemented bowl

& its deva
you wake to that
was you

in its
surge of
streaming, contained

stillness

bringing you back
drop by drop

finally standing
& then looking up...

as a voice from the terrace
calls your name.

MORMING AND EVENING

for Lorna

1

Here is the chapel,
The simple heavy door swung open
Always on its stillness -
The hewn stone altar, candlelit
Tallow and blossom smell,
And the chairs and cushions circled
Around a small low glass table
As the door shuts on some of our
Shoes left outside

To stillness. Stillness. And then as you sing
Your song about the path's narrowing
The way every word and note rings
On our listening, the last note fading
To the stillness vibrating
Its thick cool grey
Echoic twilight -
The wood of your guitar placed
Gently down - the sputtering
Of the lit match, the flame
Catching -

Its glow behind closed eyes
Each of us becoming it
Beneath the scratches, shuffles
And sighs, as we slowly, one by one, arrive.

2

Blood humming
Deep inside
Its inner sky
Behind your face
Your mind, older
Than anything

323

You can remember
The deep river
Of past and future
Connecting us here
Drawn down like
Dark threads
Out of the sunlight
Where our names
Disappear, our
Bodies, bones
Melt deeper
Than matter
Into this pulse
Rising up in each
Human form, each
Pair of eyes
Hands, face, voice
All one in this
Vast bottomless
Soul of birthing
Breathless, calm
Heart enveloped
Dawn darkness.

3

Imagine a flower. You are a mirror,
And for these moments, you have renounced speech
And so the words you would have used
To mark your seperation
Fall away, stepping through them
Through yourself -

As it closens, unresistingly
To your heart's still breath
Its petals becoming larger, clearer
Filling the mirror's space
With the endless still space
That becomes, as it is, *rose*
World given back
Its clarity and shape
Each word of it you speak

Erased into seeing -
A rose is I am

And now, in this darkened music-filled room
Images of this place turning over each other,
Screened on the wall, each intact fragment
Of its being, captured and released
Worded into sound in each plangent lingering
Chord that speaks *house, olive tree* and *vine*
In the shutter of the camera's eye that is
One picture, one word, a single length of sound
That is one breath - your eyes - closing
Under mine, moving, into each other

Till there is no other
No mirror
Only this wheeling
Unmoving centre
In which the world is
As we are, when we are.

Imagine.

4

Rainbow, a rainbow now - lying down
And feeling each colour from within
As if slowly soaking up through my clothing:
Red, from the root, like fire like wine
Its heaviness beat breathing and rising -
Orange, bathing between my legs, naked
And tender as skin licking tingling skin,
And then yellow, in the belly-eye of this body's
Energy, that is I, as it wills and survives
Green, around my chest now, budding fresh
Lucid heartfelt image of all our faces
Lightening as it spreads like the arms of a tree;
Blue, in my throat, as clear as on a mountain
Where a bird flits high transmitting this signal -
And in my mind's eye as it opens and is guided -
Indigo: pulsating silently inviolate...
Cloak of it I saw a woman swathed in, standing

With her eyes and forehead shining -
Violet, expanding beyond air beyond breath
Lifting above us in its radiant deep arch
Dazzling each colour as if through stained glass
Up into white, white fusion of dark and light
Waiting in an amphitheatre for Christ to arrive.

5

And the key
To the shadow
Is violet -
As you open the door
And it moves invisibly
Beyond you, inside you:

Sitting here,
Flooding your mind
With the colour -
Rising towards its dome
Of disembodied whiteness

Descending into this living valley
Held in the balance of a pair of open hands,
Eyes, smiling, a face
Sculpted so clear it could have been skin:

Madonna, the Black Virgin.

6

Opening to the world, floating
Centres of light all round the world tonight
United at this hour in the earth's aura
Passing invisibly across the sky
Of the countries you slowly name -
Mexico, Sweden, Norway and Germany - each name
Building its outward rippling circle
In this still pool of air as our minds
Travel there; and especially, you said
On the gently swaying deck

Of a yacht somewhere in the South China Sea,
Its sails furled in the sunset
And its cross legged helmsman
Silhouetted at the centre
Of the encircling horizon -
As this moment moves round in its shadow
And inside, in the high darkness above
Where the flicker of each dot of light
Meets across the distance as you blink -
Your voice pausing, his presence behind you
Like a stirring of leaves, and in each of us
Holding the light against the same fear
Split into phrase after phrase bleeding
Out into this deathcloud and feeding it
Till there is no way through for anyone,
The changes will never come
Our suffering will have no end -
And so to stand back, and breathe, trusting
In this one strength and vision
Of our unfolding, is the hardest thing
Because our task is to redeem
Ourselves as never before,
Through the dark pith of our being
To heal the living core
And make this step in every act and gesture
That is the day by day ground we are returning to
As we utter this prayer -
Its power forged in our will to channel
The love we have come into this depth to share
In the perfect love which casts out fear
As you spell its sound out like a mantra
And we sing this Alleluija that is yes
Our voices spread from smile to inner smile
Lightening the air above our heads
Reaching out into the night, the silence -
As somewhere you stop and look up
Drawn quietly open through a window
As its rainfall whisper touches you, ending
As we ebb back together -
And you bend to blow out this candle
To the Angel of Release.

7

And so at last
Alone, like this to say
Peace, you have come through
The healing's wordless calm
Like a cloak around you
Set down in each
Dedicated candle,
The light flickering
Behind your eyelids,
And the sound of their wicks popping
The only sound -
Not even your breathing
And this being silenced
This listening no longer in thought
Is what I mean, to be
So attuned

That the hours, the whole night
Could pass almost unnoticed
The way for a moment
I felt time stop
Between my ears until
There was nothing left
To start it again -
And then, at last
As you came out at dawn
With the core of your being
So deeply understood
You could not speak
And in that instant
As our eyes met
Your open secret
Said it all.

THE MONK

Gliding...silently...beside me, past me, vanishing - the shadow of his habit etched behind my eyes.

I cannot see his face. The hood is empty. I cannot hear his voice. It is his presence that speaks. And where we meet - on the edge of his world, and mine, in no time, I have only to close my eyes...

Darkness, and in that chill frozen place: your haunting image...numbing, emptying, like the air, me down, to the ground, in the silence, between us as you waited, aside -

- like your face, turned to one side, in profile, your features blended into darkness, hazy, unseeable, blank as this white page I draw our intersecting circles on - and then a cross, divided in black and gold -

- and then, my hand moving in a few quick strokes of charcoal - you - appearing, sketched, unmistakeably.

Sinistro. I circle your hood in gold. And ask your face to turn. And ask again. No.

Darkness. And this...invisible thread - linking us. Peering towards you. So: who are you. The question hangs, immobile...

I enter the cave, and turn to the left. A narrow passageway runs through a cleft in the wet rock. Water, through an open gap, tumbling far below. I step through.

Now I am calling for an animal. To take me to him. She flaps a little way soundlessly ahead of me, and stops - at your feet. Quite distinctly. Sandalled. In plain mediaeval leather.

Holding out my hands now. For you to take them...the hood, blurred, but the hands - touched - gently - by skin, rough textured; and then his arm lifts as he steps back, pointing over his shoulder to where the sun comes down, hooded and white, on a white horse...its light entering me...healing light...filling me

...before I turn back to go the way I have come, pausing to wrap a cloak of light around this dream-skin body as I re-emerge:

and find you, strangely, looking at the back of my neck bent as I turn, our eyes meet, dawn morning, death morning, the shape of your thighs the touch of your mouth the smell of woodsmoke your eyes burning the piled faggots blazing my hands clasped kneeling in prayer as the axe blade pulls down, blood, as my mouth plunges open and kisses the damp earth

2

Sit now. The library floor. Centre. Breathe from the heart. You sit apart and watch. We have an assignation.
          The light outside hangs still. No wind. No sounds. Not even birdsong.
          Surrounded by a circle of light -
                              - in the circle of your empty hood. In a room within a room.

Ask him to come forward now. He does. To the edge of the circle. He kneels. Silently.
          Who are you? What do you want from me? silence. His figure poised. The hands clasped. The hood dark.

Show him your talisman. And so my hand, raised, sideways, as its ringed unicorn flashes out like a thin line from between my eyes - as he stands - quickly - moving back...quivering through me...the circle intact, he cannot enter.
          But the sadness, the sadness, ebbing back towards me. The sense of shame, human, all around him, reaching through me, reaching out through me, my hands about to -
                              - but wait. It could be a trick, I don't know, I can't speak, or see, no words, feeling only, so how can I tell, hang on

Perhaps we should ask him into the circle. An elderly nun is walking past him, tears streaming down her face -
                              - as he comes in, his arms already about to embrace me, as I am him...but drawn back, out of myself...trying to get back to my body and feel...a body, under the cloth, shoulders, spine, momentarily - just show me your face - but he won't.
          Or can't. *And can I accept him whatever and whoever he is?* and I don't know, how can I, without seeing his face, then I'd know, as I nod, slowly, saying nothing to break the spell

...as a tingling begins to ripple up inside my head, as his hood slips back - white, translucent face, the eyes slightly raised, the mouth calm, the face quite independent and clear, although not young...and then fallen suddenly, the hair almost shoulder length, half covering her face as she looks down, in shadow

...and the hood dark again, standing, withdrawn, as before; as if none of this had happened, none of it

3

It deepens. There are distinctions. He closens. I do not fully understand them. Levels of being that correspond to both of us...

as the days pass.

He knows me. By knowing what I do not. And am not. Brought to the edge of the reasoning mind...on the borderline where the brain is mirrored so precisely by its own always limited, always lack of, completion...drawn beyond words into this unbounded inner sensescape where he is closer to me than I am to myself, and yet seperate, and so much freer, and accepting, destined, even -

- as he guides me: through my eyes. Up a short ramp of broken rocks out of the cave and onto a wide open expanse of plain where a long thin sandy road leads to the foot of the Tree Of Life, framing the horizon in front of which, one by one

I am taught by the Fool and his dancing, and the golden knife he places inside my tongue; and the High Priestess, in white, with the book she gave me; and the Magician, spreading his arms as a rainbow appeared behind him; and the Empress cloaking and crowning my gold covered nakedness

(while he stands apart, containing my attention)

...and drifts beside me as I revisit the region of fire, as I twist and rage and rave, and he bathes my face in a stream...as we cross to a fertile place where he pours a bucketful of red flame into the earth

and we bury what I was with a simple wooden cross, in a space between the free-standing trees

...and then deeper still, into my body: into the bloodstone root: the belly of the yellow diamond sun: the blue sapphire temple of the throat

my body's mind, become transparent - the drained bloodless corpse, ressurrected in the yellow light...energy of its scarred health confronting me...and in the bubbling inner jewelled blue fountain, my choked, black-banded throat must quench its taut thirst and strengthen

on the inside of my skin, detail by detail, written out in full. These are his words.

   This is his language.

         Scientia anima. Pro vita innatus

                          4

To the abbey. Filing, slowly, through the gate-house, and out onto the path that leads to the front of the church...as we quieten...in the bright afternoon sunlight.

         And seperate. To take it in.

Contemplatio. Sit down, folded round in its strong vibrant aura. A patch of grass around a tree stump. And then looking across at the ruined walls and arches of the outbuildings, and a small and more recent extension adjoining them, in front of which the lopped trunks of two dead concrete-and-stone-filled trees stand beside a stone slab table

And the door...into the church itself, standing open, on the darkness, down a short flight of steps

And in the darkness, a single small yellow stained glass window suspended like a keyhole...

Waiting to go in.

         Five hundred years ago. This stump fully grown. And those two trees branching, leaved with spring green.

         The sound of the builders silenced, the builders gone, you gone, and this body. And the trees and the sky, still.

Two monks, sitting at the table - one with his hand half-raised in mid-sentence - the other with his hood drawn back, the sun shining on his half-closed eyes, as he looks away to the right hearing his name called

...as you look up from the xeroxed guide brief you are holding open, and walk in through the door, glancing as you go across to where the rumbling generator hums among a short, loud exchange of voices

                         332

as the page turns. The print blurs. The monk walks, his habit and sash cord swaying, towards the entrance door, towards the window his figure shrouds, silhouetted.

Step by step. Across the ruddy stone flags. The plain vaulted ceiling reaching high above, lit by the main oculus. He stands, down in front of the window where the graphic wooden crucifix has been laid on the side altar

...my steps moving past the rows of simple backless pews, towards the cloister. Hooded. Holding a taper

the page blows backwards. The words skim. *Cistercian...masons...ordained*. Past the refectory, which is closed for repair.

The passage narrows. Trying to remember where the library was. The dormitory was...

The echo of a bell, chiming. Climbing up onto the roof level above the cloister and back out into the sunlight. A family group poses, pausing as the camera hangs, their smiles flickering...as the echo of the bell becomes sung, as it closens, leaning over, the cobblestones below, and it loudens, the slow chant spiralling upward in its serene pitched echo

quickening, to turn and go back and find it, recorded, as if it was still being sung, in the white lit museum room

and your voice saying, he was here, he stayed on after Gildas left...as we sit to sing in the church, the clear acoustic lifting up our voices like incense as you sit beside me and lightly touch my hand

...and then afterwards, watching him as he stood alone in front of the empty scaffolding, his hands by his side, his eyes closed, as the minutes passed, and a couple came in, stared at him, and then sat, near the back, together, their hands held as his stillness came into them as slowly their eyes closed -

- and twice, you turned, you said, certain that someone was standing by your left shoulder, and how you felt so calm and at one and at home

and you with your nun's face, and you with your mother superior's face, and your face, sister, and in all of our still present invisible pasts touching together

...the balance finer than a a leaf floating on the meniscus of a pool: walking this hair's breadth to where it frays, beyond air

5

Like him. That part of me. Austere. Shadow. Bookish. Cold. Reclusive. Persona. His past here, human, in me, human. On this level. Where we are one another. And why. The way I imagine him sitting I find myself sitting. Uneasily. As he images me. Physically. As close as you can get. And then closer. Timelessness embodied. Deeper than the brain. The body remembers. The sensation of rough cloth prickling skin. Later, he was mad. Later, he sat by Victorian candlelight. These parts of us. Lived. and still living. Unfinished. In this living tissue. This multi-faceted page. Of which we are the transcript. And the more, much more, connected. Not ghost. Not bound and labelled and shelved. Not dead. None of us. Million million souls. Oceanic. Incarnate. As history. Herstory. Mystory. Translinear, transtemporal. We know little. We are learning. School Of Earth. To be conscious. To be what we are, indistinct from what we have been, to hold what we may be. And what we have chosen. To suffer. To live. And manifestly love

The door is ajar. The room is unfurnished, apart from a small wooden bed and a table which is placed in front of a narrow glass window. The stone floor has been swept clean. The table is bare and wormeaten. Like the bed, it is a reasonable facsimile. Now the room is empty. I look round it once again before returning to wake up

6

'What you are experiencing with your hooded inner figure is an experience which is illustrative of the different areas which come into guidance, the different levels of experience, and the way in which these can be focussed into one particular figure'

- Gildas

His face is dark - he has many faces. His face is dark - it is rich with anticipation. His face is dark - you are journeying towards it. His face is the space of this transparency you are attempting. His face is a symbol for that scatteredness you are regathering. His face is the pain of your unknowing. His face is your death and deliverance. His face is your redemption and release. His face is the difficulty of your task. And its necessity. His face is a bead on a thread you are resonating to. His faces are yours. He is also discarnate. He has also lived. He has also known you. He remembers. For your life now. Its purpose and vocation. In what you can clearly hear and see around you, and in your voice, your face. As you know. Trust, though. Trust and accept. You are not alone and behind her taped voice as the batteries slowed, suddenly, I could hear his voice, deep and clear, speaking at normal speed...within her...as this...in the space behind the words...where this is being spoken...focussed...throat and ears reaching...far across the distance...through mist and tunnel

to where he stands, unimaginably whole

7

To the plateau. And this time, beyond. I am ready. To begin. And so again, up from the meadow, pausing to enter it fully, and sense it, before I start the walk back up the steeply curving, rising path.

 In the sunlight, walking quickly...despite the heavy boots and loaded hands. I walk the first mile in five or six seconds. Already, the plateau is looming, just as it was before. Nothing here has changed. It could even be the same day.

 A small, flat white gravelly expanse; the simple wrought iron gate and the prefab gatehouse...

I have come to meet him. The latch lifts easily. The gate opens towards me as I move back, and take the first step

...into the crown. The air immediately changing. Charged. Light. And as unbreakable as rock. Its silence. Enters me.

Cut steps, ascending. Edge of deep cloudless sky. Narrow. The breaths deepen. The street outside fades. The steps focus. My feet moving on them. Lifting, lightly...and in front of me now, a fountain rises, its thin column pitched in the air my body is becoming a part of

...undressing, to wash. Purificatio. Headfirst, head lowered, suffused, stilled, soaked in its silence. And the clothes I will wear beside it. Sandals, and a loose white robe.

 Standing in them. And then walking on up, slowly, the sky as if touching his head, and then inside it, walking up, through it. Body of light, cleansed, unnamed.

 As he closens. Pillars, up in front of him. Then the last flight, leading up to a tall wooden door, framed inside a portico. The door is closed. He waits.

Pause here.

Make your request in thought.
Consciously.
This is a place of truth.
What you ask for is given, as it is.
That is all you need to know.

Now the door, opening...candlelit...high windows, and in the centre:
a huge baptismal font.

He waits, asking.

his head light, heady, hazy   as it stirs   rising   inside him   and around

him   the tall darkness of the hood   radiating   towards him   glimpsed

accepted   and yes   unquestionably real   as this small encircled cross

hung round his neck   the circle containing him finger-drawn and crossed

in the air

Now it is enough.
It is begun.

I turn to go

LIFE MAP

1

In your beginning: that nameless, invisible, unbounded pure thing-point
of consciousness you were   you are   and to which you will return:

your whole lived life's dream dissolving, stream river ocean

and now, turning back inland, as with each step your transparent body
re-forms itself into flesh; the colour of your eyes, hair, and the clothes you
are wearing - each chosen detail that you are imaging in this precise space
of you human: in this life: at this moment: now

in the mirror of sound...listen to your name   Clara   Carole   Inge
Jane   as you speak its slow flight of breath

as it concentrates itself in each letter's shape around the blank sheet of
paper in front of you

- drawing your life's essence in your name   letting the colours come the
words come

mountain
from which I came
on this long slow descending journey
sloping down towards the valley
from its height, standing
naked and strong, in the light
bathing me in the shape
of an open golden eye

and the valley bordered by twin
steep scarps of rising pine trees
where the A stands
pointing upwards, divided
by a black cross - and I am
still not yet fully born
I am homeless in the hell of the unreal
purgatorio scenario we call world

threshold of suffering and withering

                    darkness of drugged
                     fragmented being
                     from which each
                  difficult step you make
           lies towards a living and dwelling earth
               its Y on an expanse of plain
                   containing a house
              the loop of the letter grounded
           and rooted in the soul of its greenness

                              2

Inner landscape soulscape on the inside of the mind's skin, where your
senses have travelled in each instant of your seeing

hearing and touching, tasting, smelling

- every level of reality is within you. Earth body, and body of memory;
dream body, and body of light

spiralling along each life-line in space   where the worlds touch and
overlap - collide and coalesce - in the heart of each spinning atom-earth-
world-star

now the lines that seperate the worlds are thinning   in the downflowing
light that surrounds everything

the mind can no longer hold
on this edge of its self-surpassing
to enter its fully spiritual being

element by element:

earth, that is mountain valley island tree and cave path
water, that is river lake whirlpool and sea
air, that is breeze cloud clear blue and whirlwind
fire, that is full moon sun-stream and volcano

                  mapped where the mountain's
                             M
                        is uplifted
                     into the Living Tree

                             338

- balancing sun-moon, water and fire -
- desert and green plain, day and night -

in a blue whirlpool
as it dances and descends

in the black hole
of the sun's empty pupil

and on the island ground of each aloneness

where all I have
you could fit into
a matchbox -

this dream distillation
of beaten gold:

every dream I have had
is inside it
every word I have spoken
that is real is in it
every moment of love
that was clear is still with me

and its value
and yours, and ours together
is priceless
and shining

and illimitable

3

Dross that is dust that is flesh that is grass that is you and I, that are human, channels of divinity

that is dark that is difficult that is death and sweat and shit

that is no contradiction. We are not here to waste time, we are here to learn. And suffer, and cry, and fall down, and witness the beauty and discover the wonder of being here at all, and that we belong

cycle by cycle/re-entering/each phase of your life now/to bring its spirit
fully/into your living face and eyes -

child in a garden
that child that will outlive our minds
that child that knows that nothing dies
but it becomes depth and source

(in an encircled face that became so bright it began to blind me)

as the world began to touch him and it faded,
withdrawn into unspoken privacy, drawn
face etched with its loss, sucked
towards the dragnet of blank conformity
as the fire inside it began to form

(smouldering at its lit dry green burning end)

raw anarchy of spirit on the road
in search of companions and a testament
that we are living out a mystery
our way lies through the pith of experience

(her Swiss-German face become my heart's strength)

and in each image fleeting after image
the burden shifting, each time, with recall
breakdown - bodydrained - dissolute - egodeath
the pattern detail by detail unfolding
chosen, for real, as it was and still is
but fluid from each shed skin to skin
snapshot to snapshot, like quicksilver
and as the cells of our bodies are renewed -
the layers between each symbol
revealing the centre

that is I am/and all of us/human/deepened to love/in one another as we are

returning to this life heart of earth

(in the spirit form of a man's visible face and being)

- as we reach each different present ending of this living text

and to you, as he said
how much you had come through
white-haired with your medicine eyes
and always unsure, uncertain smile
warrior in your loneliness and age
now you can hold, you can contain
peace in your innermost

self you have brought here
standing, as he spoke, and we saw you
looking out from where the river meets the sea
in a white-feathered Red Indian cloak
each rain tear fell on and rolled off
leaving you free to face the horizon
and come full circle with the setting sun

as you came round, embracing each of us
with this welling gift of your surrender.

INCARNATION

The room is divided. I see you standing, with your eyes closed, holding both your hands up at your sides

here is heaven, here is earth
choose now, either to die or be born

- and so heaven. Sitting down, with this woollen rainbow coloured shawl wrapped round me...

swathe of colours, fluid, moving, floating I sway gently from side to side, the colours reaching through me, veined and mingling and enlarging, my body limbed in every direction, swaying to meditate, to wait; circling inside between my eyes, diffuse, spreading like dye through liquid - air...calm-filled and serene...sitting on this cliff edge of air, slowly gathering this being into the memory of head, torso, legs and feet: waiting to stand and shed this cloak and - dive, down - in a long curving arc - down through the mist - down through the dark water - into this salty sea-of-flesh, and the thought of it, accepting it, although with tiredness, in the age that I am, my real age, stretching back behind me as the light gathers sky-sized and white around me on this edge, totally alone. But I know what I have come for, and I say yes

In the centre of the room are three large cushions, laid lengthways. This is the borderline

I am about to be born...

shed the shawl now come forward kneeling down, breath. breath. breath, filling what will be lungs, what will be face, arms, finding themselves stretching blindly forwards palms face down, down from my head, through it, into my body's breath mouth...going into the tunnel, wind, blowing around me him his breath beginning to roar deep inaudibly the sound all around my ears eyes nose merged together in the darkness, the warm, small tiny safety about to break open - and the pushing of breath around me, and the push-pushing filling me, inside me and between my legs drawn down into this speck of blood-bathed fruit ripening into its first fragile features; in the heart of the roar almost deafening - and I am animal on all fours, and I am fire, I am groping headlong squeezed towards air and I am parting this crack in front of me, clenched, teeth - and suddenly softening, out, released, forward belly and face across the floor now I feel them come close, those who have gone ahead of me and are waiting for me to come through just as I once remember having waited for them: soul-friends, this family beyond family, your strange familiarity as my aloneness spreads into a web of hundreds, and of years in which we have all been differently together, linked in our eyes' speech from heart to heart wherever this knowing stirs between two faces, mingling each of our presences mirrored and connected...as a hand gently touches my back, and another smooths my forehead as I touch earth flat stretched out as if fallen from a great height feeling its solid warmth ebbing up into me and feeding me the way I lay on the grass in the sun to sleep, waking as my eyes dawn open on you your face my friend as I loop this figure of eight between us from navel to navel in our smiling and shaking, soundless glad laughter -

now I turn slowly on my knees to stand seeing you down wrapped in the weight of your humanness, the pain of it spread across your parted mouth and around your head, and the sense of it severed and bleeding and from behind your eyes, feeling these hands move above your head letting the light come through me to you from the centre of both my palms, as the tears streak your cheeks, gradually slowing as it closes, and calms, inside you now, held, rocking slowly

and in you as you kick your legs and unfurl the chrysalis blanket cocooning your motionless foetal shape slowly stirring to burst into sunlit life to say *at last I am here* after sixty years *I can feel my spirit all over my body* and filling the room as we all breathed out the same yes and whooped for you

and then, as we stood, with the door of the room open, feeling the slight unsteadiness of our steps out into the hall, and into the late morning sunlight

here now:
with the valley beneath us,
trees houses road and hills
shimmering fresh through these eyes
and from each morning's
still awakening

lingering, feet touching the ground
and the seeing eye of this flesh this skin
this stardust stone

to say at last, this is our
wall-less house with its sky-roof,
this home
       this poem of pearl

              grit and bone earth.

SYMBOLIC

for Reinhold

High blue unending afternoon
Sky, above the church standing beyond
The winding road; and in the still light
As you stand on the original site
Of where the building first was - marked
On the ground by a huge stone cross
Surrounded by a circle. I watched you,
There at the apex, bearded and travel worn
And timeless, through the one life that had
Brought you to this moment. And a butterfly
Is quivering around the edges of the stones
And a crowd of kids are kicking a football
Against the wall; and one of them has wandered
Apart, suddenly alone, away from the game
He doesn't want to play, as the others
Carry on, unnoticing, the ball banging
Back as they run and shout, pushing past him;
As you stood there, still, quiet, like him
And I closed my eyes, and remembered everything.

HUMAN

for Ellen

And you lead me, stranger - smiling
Your eyes clear and open: but I am blind
To your faceless, and suddenly side by side
Touch-of-your-skin presence -
Plunged into this darkness, tunnel
You are walking me, step by step, down
As my feet shuffle, head lowered, forcing
A smile back - because the truth is
I can't, trust you yet, hang on, I tell myself
Speechlessly, half-stunned in the grip
Of this cramped, affronted animal fear
That is at your mercy, and in its wound
I am carrying and entering, shocked
By the sheer misery of it, that is mine,
My share, inside its thin-skinned covering

Trying, very slowly, to ease open and relax
As we move outside together in the sun
As I breathe its space, relieved, around me
As you sense it in your silence, guiding
My fingers along the edge of this branch
Unclenching my hand as its moistness dries
And whether it was the sound of the water
Loudening nearby, or that step you gently
Waited for my feet to steady on,
Or your caring laughter, I don't know -

Only suddenly I was free of this sickened
Self, my steps lengthened and I felt an inexpressible
Peace gathering down lighter than dust around both of us -
As I squeezed your hand to tell you, and not in words
No longer seeing you separately, outside-of-you
But inside, here, far closer than I could have known
Two unknown people could be together like this
In simple faith - and then, as I lead you
Holding your own uncertainty that I protected
In return, seeing so into your fragility
That I loved you as I would love

Any human fellow-face - unconditionally
In the pure fact of our being alive here

In this one moment we have murdered and betrayed
And only we can redeem, in the meaning
Of each word struggled with again,
As if for the first time -
Spelt out left-handed in the handwriting of a child.

WHITE MAGIC

Here is a man who I hated, and who hated me
Here is a man who tried to kill me
Who built it up, over months, inch by inch
Into the whiplash wind
He poised to strike with -
Under the mask of his warped and desperate face
That nothing but my death could solace
Nothing but the smashed image
Of my innocence could suffice: struck
Defenceless, his voice hissing down the phone
As I fell and was a shell
With a hole in its side,
Raped as the water washed over me
And left me, for dead, as I was, and in the dark
Mud sucking me naked down,
The black water ebbing round my mouth
The squeezed clear liquid
Numbing my tongue

And voiceless, veering, revengeless
Beat him up in my mind as my fists lashed back
Broke all the windows of his house
Till my own was gutted and burning,
And there was nothing I could do
Even the stone I flung out into the sea
Still had his face imprinted on it, I still wished
It was his head it would fall on from fifty feet up:
Until I came, at last, to see him as part of me
Until the pain of his being
Became enclosed deep within me,
And I was ready to invoke him, as clearly in my mind
As outside it: the man as he was and still is
Standing a matter of a few feet from me

Now I call on two figures of light
To surround him to the left and the right
Their radiance entering him
His eyes still fixed on mine -
As he turns into a snake, half-adder, half-mamba
With his tongue flickering, greased with saliva

His black pin eyes
Waiting to kill -
As he begins to dry up, withering in the light
The two figures unmoved, watching him die
As his body curls back and shrinks
And slowly is wound round
A length of wooden staff;
Stood up, in front of me,
And double-headed, intertwined
Its symbol plain as daylight:
That is to heal, and heal both of us
Within one body:

As I open my heart to take it in
Now I know the tie of hatred is broken;
And what it could be for each of us
To be freed, intact
With the whole of what we are

Given, as we have given it, back.

IN THE DARK, IN THE LIGHT

Walking the slow climb up
The old woodland path,
Leaving the crossed field
And the deserted buildings
Behind us - and the way here,
The road winding above
The land's austere exposed
Grey rock, scarred, Grecian
With its sparse bush growth
And silent with its wilderness
Opening into this green denseness
Of leaved trees with their live hollows -

Fairy, elf and gnome holes
Denizens of Pan, flitting
At the corner of our eyes, guarding
Every growing thing, in the earth-mind
Of this feminine place, they say
Take care, tread carefully, there is
Too much hard light in your eyes
You can't see us, blinded
By your intellectual sight -
And the cave high above us
Screened among the branches,
Set into the sheer cliff-rock
Its darkness we are ascending to:

Mother cave beyond patches of melting snow
Wedged three feet deep on the cut steps,
And the cross on the rockface standing
With the valley falling behind it
By the gateway with its request for silence
And plaque with its fourteen centuries of monks
Since the Magdalen died -
And time has not moved here
As we pause before its stillness
Reflected in the shuttered building
The snow has forced them down from,
And the dour, sallow-cheeked abbot
With his dog on a length of growling chain -

And the cave with its thick ivy opening
In which the sun has never shone
Its dank dewy drip-laden air, candlelit
And where a row of stained glass windows
Slick in pools of water; and the pews,
Sodden, altar and statuette icons
Loom in the imageless ancient darkness
In the body of a carved, Willendorf Venus
Head bowed to her belly, and breasts
Bowed to the darkness between her legs
We are dwarfed, peering as we walk inside
Into its cool labarynth light -

And the sound of the word *soul*
Treading the soul's ground
Standing in front of her white and sculpted,
Virgin flanked by two weaving angels
Above the thin candles flickering
Covering the deep calm of her face
Concealing what was her real face
Living her last thirty years alone here -
Closing my eyes on the white stone
As a dot of pale light began to hover
A moon that had gathered all the sun's light
As this place has the daylight inside it
Into its blood birth and death mystery

Sense that is both simultaneously
Deepened in the skin of each initiate
Come down out of the sun to reach the ground
Three jet fighters rip over, deafening
The Pieta with her lover's wounded being
Our moribund religion has betrayed -
Christ the healer, Christ the magician
Christ the lover, Christ the redeemer
Christ the heretic, Christ the human
Christ the man and Christ the woman
You honour, Hervée, with your music
As the fragile silence returns -

Kneeling on one leg as you play
With the score propped beside you
The last one, alone in the cave's depth

351

Swaying in the flickering shadow
As the notes drifted out still in earshot
As some of us stopped halfway down to listen
As it sang in the height of the air's purity
And in the tingling around our heads
We each came back to surface from:

And in the light
I walked up inside towards
From the meadow with its grazing cattle,
The landmap stretching woven below me
And then walls, roofs, streets and towers
I saw the City Of God between the mountains
Surrounded with a soft golden aura
Beneath the plateau I waited on -
With the summit invisibly in light up ahead
I went on through beyond my mind to reach

As the ground dissolved in front of me
And the light flooding entered and spoke:
In the whole texture of the land below
It pointed me down towards as I rose
And became indistinct from its seeing
(spread out from the centre within him
 that each spinning centre
 of his body became)

As the black and gold cross became crystal,
Diffused into each atom of air
Gazing into the close-up eye of a flower
Its petals unfolding their energy everywhere
As its colour space narrowed to a crack,
Full of a fleshed double-rainbow
As her open cunt became a child's face
Gazing evenly through him
As a unicorn trotted out, following
And the eye as it opened fully blazed with light
That was absolute, undiluted angel
Its radiance filling him human
In the body he slowly came back to

To stand in this well self
Feet on the ground,

352

Arms spread and eyes level
Who hath been dead and is ressurrected,
Who hath seen the living image in the being
Of every living thing -

Who is enlightened and endarkened in one.

THE THING ITSELF

Here, now, together
Standing in a circle
Come to this day's end's
Earthed calm quiet place
Our arms around each other
Breathing as one breath
Shoulder to shoulder
And legs, heads bent
As we sway - we are a tree

And I am part of you
As you are me -
Now we dance this stillness
In the night's soft shadow
Reflected on the ceiling
The music is filling
Each step, and side step
And turn - facing each other
To make this gesture:
Your hands around your heart
As you open it to me
As we spread them apart
And our eyes meet
As we sing

I love you life
And I open up my heart to you
The world becomes paradise
And I disappear

And turn, to sing again
And turn - our palms, fingers
Touched in prayer, down, as we bow
Moved to each other's
Next face and being -
The simple grace of you
Slowly overwhelming
As we enter each other
In our eyes' full standing
There is nothing to hold back

We are each saying now
What we truly mean, the one thing
We have met to say -

And the dance holds us
Enfolds us and frees us
The closer we come to letting
It shape its flow through us -
These straightforward steps
You can learn and then forget
The way you know you already know
This ease of letting go
Your hand, to take your hand

As our touch spreads
Around us and connects us
Soul to soul -
And that song you sang
As it quivers and pierces
Around me, in my throat
And behind my eyes:
Wherever you go, I shall go
Wherever you die, I shall die
And as you pass me you brush
My body like a harp -

And now, as our fingertips
Reach outstretched -
Drawn in flickering light
As the circle closes in,
Opening as our arms
Sweep back down
Our voices building
The melody heightening
The joy-sad sad-joy
Catching our throat
Ador-emus Te Dom-i-ne
Ador-emus Te Dom-i-ne
The chant cloaking us
The harmony rising
In its naked sound -
Until I know nothing
But these words as they become me -

And in the silence
We come down to
As each last note lingers

I cannot speak it anymore,
You can barely speak at all
As we stand where we are
Feeling this presence
Pulsing like a slow wind
Spreading its wings

To follow us now, forever
And to the end.

THE LAST POEM

for Kamala

Now the world
As it waits, below us
Picknicking here in the windy sunlight
Hundreds of feet high
On the tallest cliffs in Europe -
The rocks and wrecked chassis-litter below,
The boat filled curve of the harbour
The boxed white houses stretching up;
And then out to sea
Where it meets with the sky
And the silence, blue on blue,
Where the glinting water
Vanishes into formless air

And so here, poised as we sit
Emerging, alone in overselves
To go down and in among those tiny streets
In the noisy, crowded mid-afternoon of cafés
Hard kitsch tourist shops and faces
The raw heartstream of this human life
Wound on its reel of ephemeral film
Woven in the liquid density of flesh
Sleepy with sun as we cast its shadow
Down into the depth of this living dream

And on the other side -
The strange tug of the height
Leaning near the edge watching a gull fly past
Reaching beyond these eyes, to return
And be connected: but still in a part drawn
To stand here, unincluded and unspoken for
And I think of those who couldn't go on
Seeing them one by one in this figure
Plunging in his long coat with the arms splayed,
Lying back on the ground
As you hold your silver flute
And sit with the sea-sky framed around you

Blowing close - eyes closed to the light
Beating down in its brightness the notes fill
As the soul of the man lifts as he plummets
Loosens as his heart accelerates and stops
And floats, and flies, and becomes the bird's
The way your softness hovers on the wind
Its echoless silence drifting out into the blue,
The way you give your music away to the wind's breath
Knowing this whole being of earth within you
And that death is no ending
Only the last thing left we can see:

And so, having touched there, to turn
Opening our listening eyes
As you pause and it is still;
Circling back to wake and shoulder the sky
Face to face at last with being alive
In the heart of our being that must open or die
And live love to become what we are here for
Called on to be conscious
To lead, guide and heal

Through the light that shines
And dances in everything
In a grace
That enfolds it and has no more fear.

NEW AGE

for the Sisters at St Michael's Convent, Garston

'Choose life - only that and always and at whatever risk. To let life leak out, to let it wear away by the mere passage of time, to withold giving it and spreading it is to choose nothing'

- Sr. Helen Kelley

It is coming -
From high in the light where it begins
It is coming -
See the Earth rising to meet it
It is coming -
This long slow harvest of centuries
It is coming -
With a voice like the bell of a trumpet

Dawn of Aquarius, dawn of light
Bird of mid-summer hovering in the sky
Dovebird firebird angel bird
Filling the sky's circle
High across its stretched inner blue
Up above a child's uplifted face
The Earth rising towards the bird
The Earth in light turning in space
This blue pearl planet radiating light
Spinning in a single ringing note
The Earth is turning to, yearning to, returning to

Deep in this quiet place
I find my hands brought together
I hear a voice saying 'ask and receive'
I feel what it would be to doubt no longer
I see my arms opening up above my head
Holding the light in a vertical shaft of air
As it comes down flooding the silence
My skin tingling like a tuning fork
My head held back as I call out *I am here*
My body walking forwards towards a line
Coming to meet him on the other side
Where the ground breaks - and I can only jump
In faith - with nothing but this
Bared first and last self I am left with

That soul-spark I know
That invisible clear face in your face
Voice in your voice, that can trust
That can let go - and so simply
This lifelong rightness in our hearts
That can dare to say yes, it is true
I know why we are here, I can remember

I can remember the time I was grass
I can remember my first breath out of water
I can still see the starlight in your eyes
And know that you know in your innermost
Child that is stirring to reawaken us
Touched in the morning light
By the sun on the grass and the sky's clear
Blue you quicken to, dress and go out
Into this hour of Creation

Day stretching out all sun on the seed of you
Lying out on the mother ground
With nothing to do except be: the Garden
Be birdsong woodsmoke rose-smell bee-hum
Be the joy of breaking into a run
Be the wonder of taking the word flower
And watch it turn back into a flower
Into the thing it always was and is
And I am, and you are, at last - alive
Light-filled and wild
And home from home

Dawn light
River of light
Flowing into life
The light in your eyes
The light in your heart
You speak to me from
As I turn to return:
'Illuminate your life'

Now it is time to begin
To live our real lives out from within

World shadow spread across the ether
This spiral of light is descending to -
Filling your human eyes as your head bows
Where you stand on this darkening ground of air -
The Night of the World Soul swirling, suspended

Its satellite images of suffering flickering
From synapse to synapse: this last reality
Yoked, dragging its effigy out to this edge
Wheeling in the round of its crowded myriad
We were all of us one by one born to -
The wasteland we all carry only we can change
This lifeless myth we have all lived
And hardened into droning form -

And this is the gravity which holds us here
This is the paradox: every thread of this
Loom is what we have lived to weave
To come into the depth we have the only way
That has left us to finally come of age
And choose to live what we were made for -

Borderline we can only reach in time
Now the old world is beginning to die
As the light comes down into our lives
Into our days and nights and dreams

And as it comes, the shadow rises
Towards its apocalypse, the nadir
Mirroring us to ourselves in pain and rage
At the abuse and misuse - turning you
Back on yourself and your own dead skin
Sucked in to see where it also begins
And the deeper your desire reaches
The clearer you want to be, the more
The heart becomes the only real place left -

Heart born out of light and dark
And only heart that can crack the shell
Our hearts are caged in - heart we come to
As we crumble, and the shadow begins to fall
Into the cry of birth that is our soul's
Come alive as if for the first time
Each time -

God, I can feel, I can breathe
I can stand, I am - and in compassion
I can stand on fire with my heart open
I can make my pain my cleansing

I can see the shadow of my suffering

I can see the world's shadow
Becoming a rainbow - and I am
Holding this small globe between my hands
And there is light heat coming
Out from the centre of my palms
God, and my tears are shining

The rainbow needs me
The Earth my tears
The Light
This cry
Of joy!

In the dream, you said
You stood out under the stars
Filling your eyes as you slowly turned round
Alone out there in the dark that was not dark
But alive with starlight and your slow dancing
And as you moved you began to hear them sing
They filled your ears with a wave of sound
Sweeping across the face of the sky -
And one star you began to see
Drawing the sound towards itself
As it closened and brightened, you began to rise
You saw your body standing back
Your body rose around you like mist
Diving up through your arms into the air
The starlight star-sound you became
As the sky blazed with colour, streamed with colour
Flooding the length of you as you flew

And as your voice first came to me in light
Having died, you said, *right through my head*
I turn away, I turn away from death
You came like flame down into my heart
I sang your name out in light, my love
And my whole body became a heart

And now as I stand in my seeing
Under this open secret the sky is holding
In the sun behind the sun, eye behind my eyes
The sound comes down into my voice out of
That the living flame of the Word breaks through

We are the bridge where the worlds meet
We are the Spirit made manifest
Its essence the subtle form we are standing in
Reflecting the visible meaning of anything
In us, as us, and through us as it is
We are everything we have forgotten
We are here to remember and re-begin
People of God - we *are* God
When I say, my friend, I believe in you
Seeing your face in its feeling fineness
Feeling that light you have brought
Uniquely to life in each cell of you
Our being, freed from its chains, its dying
Is passionate realization - we have come
To live what is ours, to bring it through
And rise like the ground within us
Up through our hearts, heads, hands and eyes
This is a generation to end all generations
This is the place and this the time
And when I know what we can be, I am alive
I can see: we are the poem, we are its prophecy

WE ARE THE RAINBOW
SCORED ACROSS THE THUNDERCLOUD
WE ARE THE TREE OF LIFE
AND THE DESERT AROUND

WE ARE THE CAUSE
WE ARE THE SEED AND THE SEA
WE ARE THE FUTURE
WE HAVE ALWAYS BEEN

And as the scales hang in the balance
The building shakes as the air crashes past
Your voices eclipsed in the middle of the Mass
The wind rising in the bird-scattered trees
The warrior casting his arms outstretched

The healer's concentration unbroken
The child sitting silent and cross-legged
The hill where we stood in sunset silhouette

Let us pray out loud
Say it out loud
THIS IS OUR BIRTH AND OUR BREAKING
THIS IS THE CHOICE WE ARE MAKING

Atom...to molecule...molecule...to cell
Cell...to living tissue...tissue...to heart
Going into the heart...veins and capillaries
Arteries and lungs...brain and skeleton
The heart beat in me -
The heart beat beside me -
From chair to chair lined around the room
And beyond as far as each of us could reach
As I saw us standing forward in a circle
Surfacing to meet each other's eyes
Awed in the presence of who we really are here

Your voices become a wave of light
Breaking on my naked shore
A deep gold light where I walk
My feet in its ground become this ground
And all fear all aching thought all burden
Released in the clear sung calm of its strength
Seeping in through the pores of my skin -

And when it comes, when it begins
In a long horizontal flash like lightning
The Earth spins into -
At the moment of birth
Imagine
Everything gone silent
Our steps as if weightless
Our eyes without need of speech
Our minds pulsating
Our thoughts as one
Stunned act of music
Waking slowly from the grass
I am flung down onto
And meeting you

The whole of you
At last
For real
For this
And yes

We have come through.

The prophecy is now: we have work to do.
The Lovers stand with The World between them
The white heart of the rose is open
And she leans, seventeen, ageless, Virgin
Mother with the crown of her hair radiant
Swept in streaks of electric red green and gold
Holding our world to her
Inward gazing serenity -
As you cry your tears of newness, and sadness
The violin of the Passion pierces through to -
The heart that gathers and reaps you
Threshes, sifts, grinds and kneads you
Into a finer and finer wand that vibrates
In the longing we have to return and heal
The wound that is inseperable
From the duende of your song.
The Age of Light is beginning
We will see the Mind of Creation
We will meet our guides and helpers
And talk with the reality of angels -
And the way is wayless and broken and long.
Faith is the mystery, daily in this waiting
Our greatness is also that we are nothing
We are alone, we are free. To choose, risk
Renew, unendingly, life - without even knowing
What you will live to be now -
As I make my pledge and cross this line
To let go of what doesn't stand in the light
To open my heart to the will of God
To hear the born self cry I am here
All my life and death, I am here

And the summer rain falls on the grass
Behind this high screen of trees
Where you come back down to things as they are
Where it filters down like water through rock
Into the mortal earth.
And still light is bitter and unleavened,
Light is angry: is holy fire,
Full with seeing - and beyond all comprehending
Its source is almighty compassion.
And the full-leaved tree sheds its leaves
Dark red and falling -
The tiny white figure hangs
On the black cross...and you are smiling.
Wake, child, in the morning light
Wake, child, through the door into life

Barefoot on the grass, embracing you.

ACKNOWLEDGEMENTS

The quote from Frances Wickes is from *The Inner World Of Choice* (Coventure); Meister Eckhart from F.C. Happold's study and anthology *Mysticism* (Penguin); Rudolf Steiner from *On The Threshold Of The Spiritual World* (Steiner Press); Starhawk from *Dreaming The Dark* (Beacon Press); Ancient Egyptian texts from Raymond Van Over's *Sun Songs* (Mentor); C.G. Jung from *Psychology & Alchemy* (Bollingen Foundation series); AE (George Russell) from *The Candle of Vision* (Harper Colophon) Rudolf Steiner, ibid; Silver Birch, quoted by Nadia Fowler in *Tom Pilgrim: the autobiography of a spiritual healer* (Sphere Books); the *I Ching*, translated by Richard Wilhelm (Routledge & Kegan Paul); William Arkle from one of his poems in *The Great Gift* (Neville Spearman); Esther Harding from *Woman's Mysteries* (Rider); Ruth White from her discarnate guide Gildas, in a taped session with the author (1985); Alice Bailey from *A Treatise On White Magic* (Lucis Press); Raphael, transcribed by Ken Carey in *The Starseed Transmissions* (Uni-Sun); and from Sr. Helen Kelley, who is a Dominican nun.

Some of these poems were first published in the following magazines: 'Into The Depth' (*Litmus*), 'In The Mystery' (*Westwords*), 'Full Moon' (*Westwords*), 'Knowing' (*Tears In The Fence*), 'Notation' (*New Humanity*), 'Beginning' (*Gallery*), 'On Four Paintings By Frances Marsh' (*Prospice*); 'Sculpture Garden' (*The Open Poetry Conventicle*); 'Ending' (*folded sheets*); 'Sophia' (*Dada Dance*); 'Lacuna' (*Dada Dance*), 'Symbolic' (*Acumen*); and 'In The Dark, In The Light' (*Stride*). Quotations from 'The White Poem', in the context of an article ('Working Notes For The White Poem') appeared, with photographs by Carole Bruce, in *The Green Book*. Excerpts from 'New Age' have appeared in *Link Up, Metamorphosis* (the journal for the Metamorphic Association), and *Harpers & Queen*; and the poem also appears in *Transformation - the poetry of spiritual consciousness* (Rivelin Grapheme, 1988).

'The White Poem' has also been published as a seperate book with a sequence of 16 photographs by Carole Bruce (in collaboration), in a special edition by Five Seasons Press/Rivelin Grapheme Press (1988). The 'At Le Plan' sequence has also been published as a seperate book by Aquila (1988), from which the poem 'White Magic' first appeared in *The Poetry Show Anthology* (Victoria Press, 1987).

An introductory selection incorporating four poems from book 5, under the title *Raw Spiritual - Selected Poems 1980-1985* was published in 1986 by Rivelin Grapheme. It also includes photographs by Carole Bruce.

Thanks to Lizzie, Geoffrey, Carole, Katy, Tim, and everyone at Grassroots, in particular Dunstan Chan, and Geeta Nandha (the typesetter), who patiently and skilfully gave her time to the laborious process of working through a long and technically demanding text.

Finally, thanks from my heart to all my friends for their encouragement, support and understanding, both past and present, without which this journey could not have been sustained. You know who you are.

The Diamond Press two volume edition of Jay Ramsay's poem constitutes a Standard Edition. Some of the poems previously published in book form have appeared with minor errors. The versions here are definitive.

The working title for this overall and as yet unfinished work is **The Great Return**. *The sixth book, currently in preparation, is called* **Heart Of Earth**. *Please write to the Press for any further information.*